It's a Chris Fairclough sandwich as the Leeds defender is squeezed out by Arsenal's Ian Wright and Kevin Campbell

Published by

ipcmagazines

Distributed by IPC Marketforce

£3.95

IAN WRIGHT

He could be the new Gary Lineker

WITH Gary Lineker stepping out of the international scene, the search is on for his replacement - the man who'll carry the goalscoring burden for England in the next World Cup.

You could say Graham Taylor is spoiled for choice as he looks for the man to take over the goalscoring burden.

In Ian Wright, Alan Shearer and David Hirst, England's future looks to be in good hands. All are prolific goalscorers capable of striking from any range.

"Gary Lineker's retirement should not present a major problem," says the England boss, knowing that even if Wright, Shearer and Hirst fail to live up to expectations, Brian Deane and Wright's exciting team-mate Kevin Campbell are waiting in the wings.

Wright has the most experience, and that probably makes him the favourite to fill Lineker's golden boots.

Dismal

The goals have always flowed from the 28-year-old Londoner. His predatory instincts in the penalty area brought him better than a goal a game south of the River Thames with Crystal Palace and he continued in the same vein north of it with Arsenal - in spite of The Gunners' dismal season.

Even at £2.5 million, Arsenal boss George Graham knew he had landed a bargain. Yet Graham is careful with his praise, never allowing his players to get carried away, even if they can score four goals in one game.

"Ian is one of the quickest players I've seen but he can improve his touch and in holding up the ball," says Graham. "He is lucky to be part of a very exciting forward line. He is a brave player who gets into dangerous areas

OR ENGLAND!

Graham Taylor

Alan Shearer is very much in the Lineker mould

David Hirst – all power and skill

but he must learn to channel his aggression.

"Ian's generally a level-headed and sensible boy thankful for all that's happening to him after he came into the professional game so late."

"He shows the enthusiasm of a 20-year-old in training and is a lovely player to work with."

Arsenal know all about Shearer. On his full debut for Southampton as a 17-year-old he rattled in a hat-trick as The Saints stunned The Gunners.

A Geordie lad with his feet planted firmly on the ground, Shearer has in common with Lineker the professional attitude that can add an extra dimension to an international hopeful's prospects.

Then there is his speed, vision and goalpoaching instinct - he's already the highest-ever scorer for the England Under-21 side.

What of the third member of the leading candidates for this highly responsible position?

Taylor assess Hirst this way: "He gets Lineker-type goals in the six-yard area but he can also hit the ball tremendously hard from 15 yards. The lad has a lot going for him."

Campbell burst into the reckoning at Highbury in dynamic style last season, but Taylor feels he has yet to see the finished product.

"He is a tremendous runner with the ball and this takes the eye. But we must get a better end product."

But for Campbell, and for England fans everywhere, it's clear that the best is yet to come.

Bryan Robson
MANCHESTER UNITED

KOP

McManaman won England honours before his big-time Liverpool debut

LIVERPOOL had their ups and downs last season but the future looks to be in safe hands, with the emergence of Steve McManaman, destined to step into Ian Rush's shooting boots.

Mike Marsh strikes against Auxerre

McManaman was earmarked for stardom even before he had made his full debut for Liverpool. The kid with the long, loping stride has the ability to pressure defenders into mistakes.

As he learned his craft as the sorcerer's apprentice last season, so his goal-poaching ability improved, too. The phenomenal crop of injuries at Anfield meant that McManaman was perhaps brought along too soon.

But having been thrown in at the deep end, he quickly learned to swim.

Perfecting his craft alongside Rush, the kid is now ready to take over from him, and that's something Steve's well prepared for.

as well as any adult, and all that's missing is the ability to handle the physical side of the game."

Tall and skinny, McManaman is likely to 'fill out' and add strength over the next couple of seasons

THIS!

Steve McManaman - an England star of the future?

Many young players would find the superstar tag a distraction but it's a burden that barely seems to bother the super-confident lad who earned the nickname Shaggy because of the long, thick hair he trimmed after making the breakthrough to the big time.

Last season's injury crisis at Anfield propelled superkid Steve, who grew up an Everton fan, to stardom well ahead of schedule. But he definitely has a head for the heights.

Don't mistake his supreme confidence for cockiness. It's just the magic ingredient that will help him reach the top and should make him an England star of the future.

Lawrie McMenemy gave McManaman his debut for the England Under-21s before the youngster had even started a first-team match for Liverpool.

"He has an old head on young shoulders," says Reds boss Graeme Souness of his protege. "He handles himself

as he builds on his growing reputation before the Kop.

The rest of the First Division has already had a glimpse of the youngster's blossoming talent, but his best is yet to come.

McManaman wasn't the only discovery to break into the big time during The Reds' troubles last season.

The question on many lips around Anfield last term concerned the successor to Ronnie Whelan, whose career was threatened by a serious knee injury. Kirkby kid Mike Marsh took up the gauntlet with a series of solid performances.

By the time he scored the second goal, his first-ever for the senior team, in Liverpool's epic UEFA Cup comeback against Auxerre with a powerful header, he had already made himself a popular figure with the Kop.

Now he seems destined to join John Aldridge, Gary Ablett and Steve McMahon as Scousers who made good in the famous red shirt.

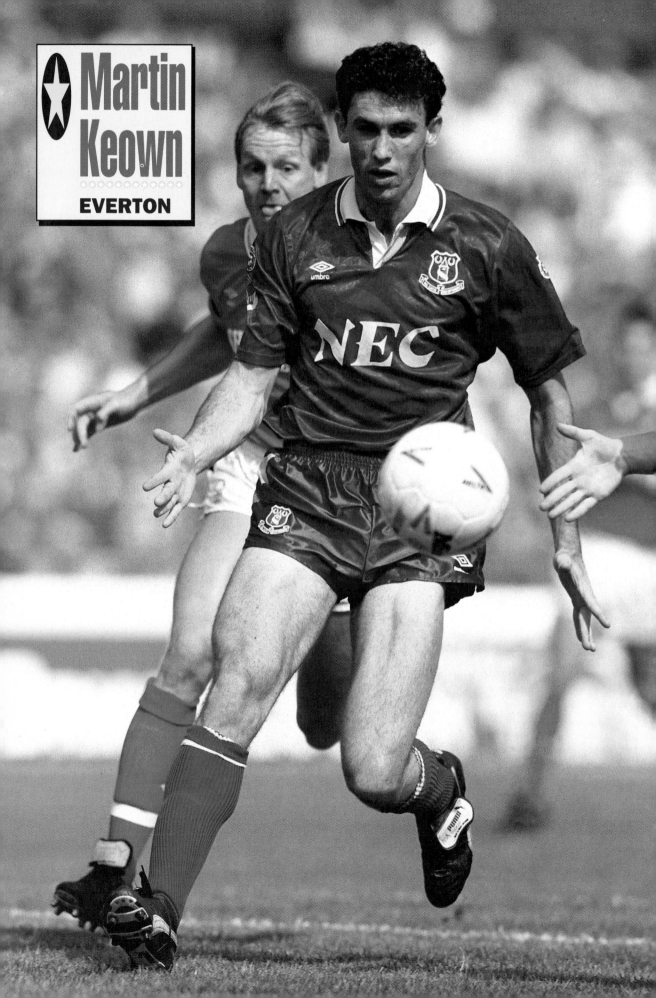

Martin Keown

★

EVERTON

MASTER STRIKER

IF goalscoring is an art, then John Aldridge must be a master craftsman.

As First Division managers offer outrageous sums for unproven strikers, John King made the smartest move of all last season. He brought Aldridge to Prenton Park for a mere £250,000 from Real Sociedad - and Aldo ended up the League's leading scorer.

Journeyman John has done the rounds, and the move to Merseyside brought his career full circle. From South Liverpool to Newport to Oxford, on to Anfield then back across the Mersey via Spain, Aldo has always done the business.

So what is it that keeps John popping up in the penalty area for a tap-in, rifling the ball home from 12 yards or rising above his marker to nod the ball home? He has the magic touch all right, and puts it all down to instinct.

"I've always said that the secret to goalscoring is instinctual," says John. "There really is no other way to explain it.

Aldridge sets Liverpool on their way to FA Cup Final success against Everton in 1989

"I think that if you asked any successful striker they would tell you the same thing. It's a matter of good timing, knowing when to move for the ball.

"You get into the area at the right moment, shake off the defender and you're away."

All sounds so simple, doesn't it? But then that's Aldo - nothing too fancy or complicated - just goals.

The most expensive buy Rovers have ever made in their 106-year history, but he's been great value for money. Having passed the 300-goal mark, he's now going for 400, and sees no reason not to set targets just because he's reached the ripe old age of 33.

Former Kopite John hopes to pass that target in the Premier Division, and who knows, he could even get a goal or two in front of the Kop.

"The fans have always been great towards me at Anfield, so has everyone on the staff there," says John. "And I know they'd take it the right way if I did score against The Reds."

He's played at compact grounds that back on to railway sidings and before 80,000 crowds in Barcelona, in the World Cup for Ireland and through all four divisions – everywhere he's been, he's scored goals regularly.

Aldo proved to be a real bargain at Tranmere

"I suppose taking it all into account I'm most proud of my time in Spain," says the striker. "I went over there and succeeded where a lot of other players from this country have failed.

"When I finally call it a day and look back, I'll consider that my finest accomplishment."

BIG CITY RIVALS

Who are top dogs after a decade of derbies?

Between 1981 and 1991 Liverpool never fell out of the top two in the First Division.

And for five years in the middle of the decade, the two Merseyside giants took it in turn to lift the League title.

When Liverpool relinquished their grip in 1985 it was Everton who were there to make sure the trophy didn't venture far - and the mighty Reds made sure it was back at Anfield a year later.

But while Everton were unable to stay at the top after the departure of Howard Kendall to Spain, Liverpool continued to dominate under Paisley, Fagan and then Dalglish.

As if to underline Liverpool's superiority, Everton managed to win just four of the 20 Merseyside derbies.

THE RESULTS

	At Anfield (L'Pool first)	At Goodison (Everton first)
1981-82	3-1	1-3
1982-83	0-0	0-5
1983-84	3-0	1-1
1984-85	0-1	1-0
1985-86	0-2	2-3
1986-87	3-1	0-0
1987-88	2-0	1-0
1988-89	1-1	0-0
1989-90	2-1	1-3
1990-91	3-1	2-3

Glasgow

Just like the City of Glasgow itself, the fortunes of Celtic and Rangers during the 1980s were split right down the middle.

While the first half of the decade undoubtedly belonged to the men in green and white, the Light Blues emerged from the doldrums with a vengeance under Graeme Souness.

Not only did Souness revolutionise Rangers, he transformed Scottish football as a whole and injected interest in a game which, by the admission of many, had gone stale.

Four title wins in five years for the Ibrox club made up for the disappointment earlier in the 80s when Rangers finished as low as fifth in the Premier League at one stage.

Like Souness, Celtic boss Liam Brady enjoyed a successful and lucrative career as a player in Italy, but whether he can revive the Parkhead club the way Souness revitalised Rangers is another matter.

THE RESULTS

	At Parkhead (Celtic 1st)	At Ibrox (Rangers 1st)
1981-82	3-3/2-1	0-2/1-0
1982-83	3-2/0-0	1-2/2-4
1983-84	2-1/3-0	1-2/1-0
1984-85	1-1/1-1	0-0/1-2
1985-86	1-1/2-0	3-0/4-4
1986-87	1-1/3-3	1-0/2-0
1987-88	1-0/2-0	2-2/1-2
1988-89	3-1/1-2	5-1/4-1
1989-90	1-1/0-1	1-0/3-0
1990-91	1-2/3-0	1-1/2-0

FLASHBACK
Rangers 5 Celtic 1
Aug.27, 1988

Having won the League and Cup double in their centenary year Celtic came crashing down to earth during the 1988-89 season - losing three of the four Premier meetings with Rangers. Their worst defeat was at Ibrox at the start of the season when Rangers scored five goals in this fixture for only the third time in a century.

FLASHBACK
Everton 4 Liverpool 4
Feb.20, 1991

While League clashes between the two great rivals have been dour affairs, the same could not be said of the 4-4 draw in the FA Cup at Goodison - a game described by some as the best ever seen. The goals flowed like wine in the second highest scoring derby of all time. And the surprises continued - days later Kenny Dalglish resigned.

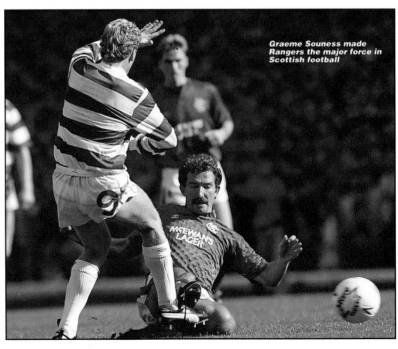

Graeme Souness made Rangers the major force in Scottish football

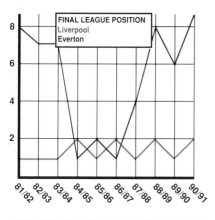

FINAL LEAGUE POSITION
Liverpool
Everton

81/82 82/83 83/84 84/85 85/86 86/87 87/88 88/89 89/90 90/91

BIRMINGHAM

Not even the staunchest Birmingham fan could argue that his team has played anything but second fiddle to Aston Villa down the years.

And, while the season just past has seen something of a Blues' revival, Birmingham are still a long way off competing on equal terms with Ron Atkinson's men.

Perhaps it's worth remembering, however, that Villa once suffered the indignity of Third Division football but recovered to claim another League title.

Under Graham Taylor, Villa finished second to Liverpool in 1990 but lost their way again under Jo Venglos.

With Atkinson at the helm the glory days are surely on their way back to Villa Park. At St.Andrews, the wait may be longer.

THE RESULTS

	At Villa Park (Villa first)	At St.Andrews (Blues first)
1980-81	3-0	1-2
1981-82	0-0	0-1
1982-83	1-0	3-0
1983-84	1-0	2-1
1985-86	1-0	0-0
1987-88	0-2	1-3

FLASHBACK
Birmingham 3 Villa 0
Dec.27,1982

The Christmas crunch between the two West Midlands rivals attracted almost 44,000 to St.Andrews - Birmingham's biggest gate of the season. And the Blues' fans weren't to be disappointed as their side won 3-0 with goals from Noel Blake, Ian Handysides and Mick Ferguson.

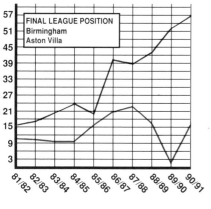

FINAL LEAGUE POSITION
Birmingham
Aston Villa

81/82 82/83 83/84 84/85 85/86 86/87 87/88 88/89 89/90 90/91

NORTH LONDON

Spurs' FA Cup Semi-Final win over Arsenal in 1991 may have been music to the ears of Tottenham fans, but it only went a little way towards atoning the Gunners' dominance in recent years.

Two title wins in the space of three years - the first recorded in such dramatic fashion on the last day of the 1988-89 League season - restored pride within the marble halls of Highbury.

They stirred up only hatred and jealousy a few miles away at White Hart Lane, however, where Spurs continue to be classed as 'a good Cup side with no chance of winning the League'.

Last season, perhaps, saw a turning point for both clubs; Spurs were saved from financial ruin and Arsenal found out just how tough it is to defend the League Championship.

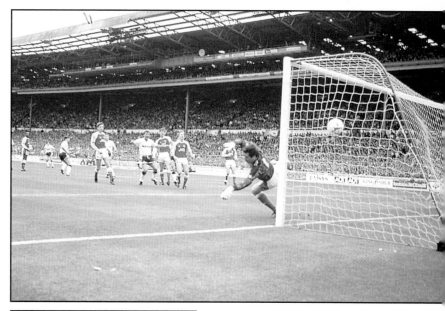

EDINBURGH

The 1980s was a miserable decade for Hibs - in derby terms at least.

At Tynecastle they managed just one victory and celebrated only two triumphs over their great rivals at Easter Road.

It was a decade of unprecedented success for Hearts who finished runners-up in the Premier on three occasions.

But there was also disappointment for the Jam Tarts, notably in 1986 when the title was snatched from them on the last day and they also lost the Scottish Cup Final.

THE RESULTS

	At Tynecastle (Hearts first)	At Easter Rd (Hibs first)
1983-84	3-2/1-1	1-1/0-0
1984-85	0-0/2-2	1-2/1-2
1985-86	2-1/3-1	0-0/1-2
1986-87	1-1/2-1	1-3/2-2
1987-88	1-0/0-0	2-1/0-0
1988-89	1-2/2-1	0-0/1-0
1989-90	1-0/2-0	1-1/1-2
1990-91	1-1/3-1	0-3/1-4

THE RESULTS

	At Highbury (Arsenal first)	At White Hart Lane (Spurs first)
1981-82	1-3	2-2
1982-83	2-0	5-0
1983-84	3-2	2-4
1984-85	1-2	0-2
1985-86	0-0	1-0
1986-87	0-0	1-2
1987-88	2-1	1-2
1988-89	2-0	2-3
1989-90	1-0	2-1
1990-91	0-0	0-0

FLASHBACK
Spurs 3 Arsenal 1
April 14, 1991

Who will ever forget Paul Gascoigne's free-kick opener in this thrilling FA Cup Semi-Final? That set Spurs on the way to victory with Gary Lineker grabbing two goals either side of Alan Smith's reply for Arsenal.

FLASHBACK
Hibs 0 Hearts 3
Sept.15, 1990

Coming at a time when Hearts chairman Wallace Mercer was trying to instigate a merger between the two clubs, tension was running high in this Edinburgh derby. Hearts won comfortably, but the game was marred when John Robertson was attacked by a Hibs supporter after his 12th minute opener and a pitch invasion ensued.

Hearts have dominated Hibs in recent years

Mark Hughes' spectacular strike couldn't stop United collapsing 5-1 against City

Peter Beardsley enjoyed a Happy New Year in 1985

NORTH EAST

It was just like old times last season as Newcastle and Sunderland made the football headlines.

The St James' Park club was the first to hit the back pages when Kevin Keegan shocked the soccer world by taking over as manager of the club he revitalised as a player in the early 80s.

His appointment as successor to Ossie Ardiles thrilled the fans who are now sure the good times are just around the corner.

For Sunderland, last season was even more memorable.

The Roker men became the first Second Division club for ten years to reach the FA Cup Final as Wearside went crazy.

John Byrne was the hero, scoring in every round to take Sunderland into the Final, including the winner in the Semi against Norwich.

Could it be then that the North-East giants are at last set to emerge from the slumbers of recent years?

THE RESULTS

	At St.James' Park	At Roker Park
	Newcastle 1st	Sunderland 1st
1984-85	3-1	0-0
1989-90	1-1	0-0

FLASHBACK
Newcastle 3 Sunderland 1
Jan. 1, 1985

The New Year's Day fixture was a personal triumph for Peter Beardsley who delighted the 36,000 crowd with a stunning hat-trick. For Sunderland it was another crippling blow in a disappointing season which ended with the Milk Cup finalists being relegated from the First Division.

MANCHESTER

The 1990-91 season saw the balance of power in Manchester swing, albeit briefly, back in City's favour.

They finished fifth in Division One, one place above United, but the Old Trafford club bounced back in style last term.

Under Alex Ferguson, United have restored some of the pride and reputation built up during the legendary Busby era.

Fergie hasn't just a built a team of winners, but of entertainers too - just like his Maine Road counterpart, Peter Reid.

After a lean time by their own high standards City are also back up there challenging for the major honours.

Can Manchester now succeed Merseyside as football's capital?

THE RESULTS

	At Maine Road	At Old Trafford
	City 1st	United 1st
1980-81	1-0	2-2
1981-82	0-0	1-1
1982-83	1-2	2-2
1985-86	0-3	2-2
1986-87	1-1	2-0
1989-90	5-1	1-1
1990-91	3-3	1-0

FLASHBACK
City 5 United 1
Sept. 24, 1989

Alex Ferguson's job was on the line at the time his £12m side was thrashed by City's young team. Goals by David Oldfield, Ian Bishop and Trevor Morley saw City race into a 3-0 lead and, while a spectacular Mark Hughes volley put United back in with a shout, further strikes by Oldfield and Andy Hinchcliffe completed the rout.

NOTTINGHAM

County boss Neil Warnock admits that Brian Clough is his managerial idol. And it's true, the two do share certain characteristics.

But, while similarities may be apparent in their style of work, it's unlikely that Warnock will ever match Cloughie's achievements while he remains at Meadow Lane.

Unlike the cashflow situation at the City Ground, money is not thrown about with such gay abandon on the other side of the River Trent where Warnock has had to operate on a shoestring budget.

The fact he put County up there in the top flight, battling it out with Forest and the other big guns was an achievement in itself. But it's unlikely the Warnock success story will continue - as far as County are concerned at least.

Forest, meanwhile, for all Clough's genius and man-management skills have had a relatively lean time in the League of late - although they haven't slipped out of the top ten for a decade.

They have enjoyed unprecedented success in Cup competitions, but it's the League title which Cloughie covets.

He steered Forest to the Championship in 1978 and is likely to remain at the helm for another two years in the hope that he can repeat that feat.

And then who knows what will happen to Forest - Neil Warnock to take over perhaps?

THE RESULTS

	At Meadow Lane County 1st	At the City Ground Forest 1st
1981-82	1-2	0-2
1982-83	3-2	2-1
1983-84	0-0	3-1

FLASHBACK
Forest 3, County 1
Oct.16, 1983

County were desperately trying to keep their feet off skid row at this stage - and Forest showed them little or no mercy. After just three seasons in the top flight, County were on their way down and Forest did little to help with goals from Ian Wallace, Ian Bowyer and Peter Davenport giving them a comfortable victory. Trevor Christie replied for County who had David Hunt and Justin Fashanu sent off to complete a miserable day their fans will want to forget.

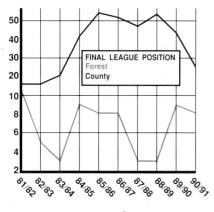

FINAL LEAGUE POSITION
Forest
County

81/82 82/83 83/84 84/85 85/86 86/87 87/88 88/89 89/90 90/91

SHEFFIELD

Two of the games most charismatic managers helped put Sheffield soccer back on the map - Ron Atkinson and Dave Bassett.

Although Big Ron left under acrimonious circumstances after guiding Wednesday back to the big time (not to mention a Wembley triumph in the Rumbelows Cup) the foundations for a bright future had already been laid.

The players, the style of play, the passion, the support - the good times have returned to Hillsborough, and Trevor Francis has carried on the restoration work begun by Atkinson.

Across the steel city, meanwhile, Dave Bassett was producing miracles of his own at Bramall Lane where he took The Blades from the Third Division to the First in successive seasons.

The two Sheffield clubs have rarely appeared in the same division over the past 20-odd years and last season (1991-92) saw the first League meeting between the once powerful pair for more than a decade.

Back in 1979, a THIRD DIVISION clash between the city rivals attracted a crowd of almost 50,000 - a figure which underlines the potential in the soccer mad city of Sheffield.

THE RESULTS

	At Hillsborough Owls 1st	At Bramall Lane Blades 1st
1970-71	0-0	3-2
1979-80	4-0	1-1
1989-90	ZDS Cup 2nd Round 3-2	

FLASHBACK
Wednesday 3 United 2
Nov.21, 1989

The first Sheffield derby for a decade took place at Hillsborough in the ZDS Cup - a minor cup match but a big occasion for the fans of the steel city who turned out in their thousands. Although Wednesday were to suffer the indignity of relegation from the First Division while United won promotion from the Second, it was The Owls who triumphed on the night thanks to an extra-time winner by John Sheridan. Wednesday goals by Dalian Atkinson and Carlton Palmer had earlier been cancelled out by Brian Deane and Bob Booker.

John Sheridan was the Wednesday hero against United in the ZDS Cup clash in 1989

FACTS &

SHOOT's A-Z of football... Part 1

ABBEY STADIUM, home of Cambridge United, is not the most popular ground to visit these days. The club's long ball game is, so some say, not a pretty sight. Attitudes, it seems, haven't changed that much from the time Cambridge were first elected to the League and a supporter was quoted as saying: "League football in Cambridge is like having bingo in the Albert Hall." Wonder what he'd make of Premier League football in Cambridge?

BOB STOKOE found fame as a manager when he led Second Division Sunderland to a memorable FA Cup Final triumph over mighty Leeds in 1973 - but he also deserved a medal for what he did at Rochdale five years earlier. In an effort to rebuild an ailing side he gave 11 players free transfers, sold Les Green to Derby for £8,000 and with the cash bought: nine new players, four sets of team strip and a fresh coat of paint for the ground.

CHARLES Burgess Fry must be one of the world's greatest-ever all-round sportsmen. A right-back for Southampton in the 1900 Cup Final, he was also capped for England against Ireland in 1901. He represented Oxford University at cricket and football - and also held the WORLD long jump record. In addition he played cricket for Surrey, Sussex, Hampshire and England and also represented his country in athletics.

Charles Burgess Fry

DOUBLE-winning manager Bill Nicholson was renowned more for his success as a boss than as a player - but he did boast something of a unique claim to fame before hanging up his boots to lead Spurs through their greatest era. On May 19, 1951 he made his one and only appearance for England...and scored with his very first kick in the 5-2 Wembley victory over Portugal.

ENGLAND's first match under Alf Ramsey - against France in 1963 - was a disaster for the new boss... England lost 5-2. It was also a nightmare 'England debut' for a Daily Mail reporter who, as he began to dictate his five page story over the phone, could only watch in horror as the wind blew four of the completed pages away. The one page he salvaged began...'in the 72nd minute of the match....'

FOOTBALL legend Pele holds the record (professional) for scoring the most goals in a season. In 1959 he scored a staggering 126 goals for Santos and Brazil...in 103 games. Another Brazilian, Arthur Friedenreich, holds the record for the most goals in a career - 1,329 over a 26-year period between 1909 and 1935.

GORDON BANKS made some memorable saves for England during a distinguished international career (who could forget that sensational stop from Pele in 1970?) but in one match against Malta in May, 1971 he wasn't called on to make a single save in the whole 90 minutes. In fact he didn't receive the ball from a Maltese player during the match, he fielded only back passes. England won 5-0.

On the spot – Palace against Brighton in 1989

FUNNIES

Martin Buchan completes a Cup double with Manchester United in 1977

Il Nicholson one game one goal

INSPITE of being the First Division's leading scorer with 21 League goals, Southampton striker Mick Channon was still unable to save The Saints from relegation at the end of the 1973/74 season. The same fate befell Bob Hatton four years later when he was top scorer in Division Two with 22 goals, but it wasn't enough to prevent Blackpool slipping into Division Three.

JOE LOUIS, the internationally acclaimed boxer of the 1930s and 1940s, won the World Heavyweight Championship in 1937 and retained it until his retirement eleven years later. But what is not so widely known about this boxing legend is that he signed amateur forms for Liverpool in 1944.

KELVIN Morton, a top referee from Suffolk, holds the dubious record of awarding the most penalties in a game (outside a shoot-out). On March 27, 1989 he awarded Crystal Palace four spot-kicks and Brighton one in their Second Division match at Selhurst Park. Palace only managed to convert one, as did Brighton, but The Eagles ran out 2-1 winners.

LONGEST game of football on record lasted three and a half hours and was a Libertadores Cup match between the Brazilian club Santos and the Uruguayans of Penarol. The game kicked off at 9.30 on August 2, 1962 and, because the teams agreed to play to a finish to achieve a result, it didn't end until 1am the following morning...when they decided to call it a day at 3-3!

MARTIN BUCHAN is the only man to skipper both Scottish and English FA Cup winning teams. He was Aberdeen captain when they won the Scottish Cup in 1970 and he skippered Manchester United to Wembley triumph against Liverpool in the English equivalent seven years later. It was the Scot's second FA Cup Final appearance as a year earlier United had lost to Southampton. When once asked by a journalist 'Could I have a quick word, Martin?' the dry-witted Scot replied 'velocity' and walked off.

HAT-TRICK heroes Bill Poyntz of Leeds and Billy Holmes of Southport hold the distinction of scoring three goals (Poyntz against Leicester in 1922; Holmes against Carlisle in 1954) on the day they were married - the only Football League players to achieve such a feat on their special day.

* Now turn to page 38 for the rest of SHOOT's A-Z of soccer facts and funnies.

Shoot's magnificent seven reveal all ⭐

QUESTIONS	Steve McManaman (Liverpool)	Ian Baird (Hearts)	Jimmy Carter (Arsenal)
Which current footballer do you most admire?	John Barnes - he's got so much skill and strength. A buzz goes up at Anfield every time he gets the ball.	Gianluca Vialli of Italy - he's the complete centre-forward. He works hard and scores spectacular goals.	David Rocastle - I used to pick ideas up from watching him play on the wing before he switched to midfield.
What are your worst faults as a player/person?	Defending and not tackling back.	I get frustrated very easily. Generally, I'm too impatient.	I really must improve my heading. At home I'm too lazy.
Who is the wackiest person you have met in football?	Steve Nicol or David Speedie - they both like to lead the sing songs.	Vince Hilaire - we roomed together on away trips for two years at Leeds. He's great fun to be with.	Former England coach Steve Harrison who I worked with at Millwall. A genuinely funny man.
If Jim could fix it for you, what would you ask?	To score a hat-trick in a Merseyside derby.	Play snooker with Steve Davis and golf with Nick Faldo.	Win the pools so I could buy my dad a house.
Outside football, what is your claim to fame?	I was the North West schools cross country champion.	I once parachuted out of a plane for charity. I'd taken flying lessons before but was still petrified.	I went to the same school in Stoke Newington as Top of the Pops DJ Tony Dortie.
Which TV programme do you love/hate?	Love: The Young Ones/ Hate: Emmerdale Farm.	Love: Dallas and Cheers/ Hate: Neighbours and Home and Away.	Love: Any sport programmes/ Hate: Any Australian soap.
What do you do away from football?	Rest, listen to music, play pool or golf	I love taking my German shepherd dog 'Rocky' for walks and then putting my feet up.	Relax, watch TV and play football with my son Luke.

THE STARS

Rick Holden (Oldham)	Keith Curle (Man.City)	Gerry Creaney (Celtic)	Dion Dublin (Cambridge)
Chris Waddle - he's always refused to change his style of football.	Des Walker because of his pace and ability to read the game.	Ian Rush has a phenomenal goalscoring record, but Kenny Dalglish was the most complete player I've ever seen.	Chris Waddle - you expect something to happen every time he's on the ball.
I get frustrated too easily and lose concentration. I hate weekend drivers in the Dales.	As a player, my heading could be better. Away from football I'm an impatient driver.	My heading could improve and I'm not too proud of my quick temper either.	I'm not selfish enough in front of goal and when I'm out I buy too many rounds of drinks!
My old Halifax team-mate Phil Brown, now Bolton. He once got the runaround from Eddie McGoldrick and when Eddie's boot came off, Phil threw it in the crowd.	Gary Megson. A combination of tweed flat cap, beige bomber jacket, ten-year-old brown cords and black shoes is as wacky as you can get.	Certainly nobody at my club. They haven't got a decent sense of humour between them.	The former Cambridge striker George Reilly - he's a rascal with the deep heat.
Mend my Dad's scooter.	Not to be bow-legged. If I had straight legs, I'd be 6ft 7ins instead of six foot.	For me to steer clear of serious injury and enjoy health and happiness when I retire from football.	To play basketball with the Chicago Bulls star Michael Jordan.
When I was 14 I took three wickets with my first three balls in senior cricket.	When I was at Wimbledon, Lawrie Sanchez bought me a drink!	My cousins are Greg and Pat Kane of the pop group Hue and Cry.	My team-mates reckon I own the worst pair of shoes in the world because they are square-toed and make me look like Frankenstein.
Love: Blackadder and Laurel and Hardy films/ Hate: Any soap - especially those made in Australia.	Love: Cheers/ Hate: Party Political broadcasts.	Love: Most sports and comedy programmes/ Hate: Prisoner Cell Block H.	Love: Bill Cosby in the Cosby Show/ Hate: Anything with Rik Mayall.
I like listening to music, playing sport and reading - I'm currently taking a physiotherapy course at University.	Spend time with my two children, Thomas and Natalie, and play golf.	I usually go for a game of golf and then pick my little brother up from school.	I enjoy listening to jazz music or watching videos in front of a log fire.

No.1: LIAM BRADY

The Irish midfield genius loved life in Italy - and it's fair to say the Italian paying public loved him...wherever he played.

When Brady quit Arsenal in the summer of 1980 - a year after he'd been voted the PFA Player of the Year - it was Juventus who were to benefit from his silky midfield skills.

In his first season with the Turin giants Brady didn't miss a game and scored eight League goals as Juventus romped away with the Championship.

Two years later he teamed up with Trevor Francis at Sampdoria before joining Inter Milan and, finally, winding up his career in Italy with Ascoli.

Brady lived, ate and breathed Italian football *(just as David Platt promises to do)* and his dedication paid dividends.

No.2: MARK HATELEY

One goal for England in Brazil was all it needed to convince AC Milan that Hateley (above) was the man for the toughest Italian job of all.

A striker's lot is not always a happy one on the continent (just ask Ian Rush, Luther Blissett, Jimmy Greaves and Co) but the man they called 'Attila' was equal to the task.

He wasn't a prolific goalscorer - he averaged one in every three games - but his aerial power made him feared by opponents and revered by his adoring public.

And, but for a cruel spate of injuries, his spell with Glenn Hoddle at Monaco would have been as rewarding as his Italian adventure.

HE BEST

itish hits abroad

No.4: GARY LINEKER

The England hit-man wasn't treated by Barcelona coach Johan Cruyff with the respect his scoring record deserved.

His best spell with the Spanish legends was under Terry Venables, the man who took Lineker (left) and Mark Hughes to the Nou Camp for a combined fee of £5m.

While Hughes struggled to come to terms with the demands of the fickle Spanish public, Lineker proved value for money - until the departure of Venables.

When Cruyff took over, England's greatest ever goalscorer found himself in an accustomed role on the right wing. It didn't stop him playing a part in the European Cup-Winners' Cup success enjoyed by the Catalans, however.

No.5: TREVOR FRANCIS

Like his one-time Sampdoria team-mate Liam Brady, Francis took to Italy like a teenage Geordie to Newcastle Brown.

But his appearances, and his effectiveness, were forever restricted by injuries. His England career also suffered as a result.

Just one of his five years in Italy - four with Sampdoria and one with Atalanta - passed uninterrupted. But his dashing forward play and willingness to take opponents on made him a crowd favourite.

And, while the statistics state that he managed just 18 goals in 89 League appearances, his services were still in demand when he quit the Italian scene to join Glasgow Rangers in 1987.

No.3: JOE JORDAN

The Italians probably hadn't seen anything quite like the Scottish mean machine.

One thing's for sure; defences in the English First Division weren't sorry to see the back of the former Leeds and Manchester United tormentor.

His power in the air and fearlessness in the challenge made him an instant hit with the AC Milan fans. Jordan's gap-toothed grin, snarl more like, earned him the suitable nickname of The Shark.

It's safe to assume that, in Mark Hateley a few years later, Milan saw Jordan Mk II.

The big striker (below) later joined Verona before returning to Britain to enter the field of management where his never-say-die qualities are already in evidence.

Despite a string of injuries, Francis was a big hit in Italy

No.6: PAUL ELLIOTT

Elliott was a lone British figure in the Italian First Division for a time - and he flew the flag superbly.

'Foreign' defenders are a rare import in Italy where stoppers and sweepers are usually cultivated on home soil.

And it says a lot for Elliott (right) that, even in a struggling Pisa side, he built a sound reputation for handling some of the best strikers in the world.

After two seasons abroad he provided similar resistance in the Celtic back line and is currently holding the Chelsea defence firm. Incredibly, international honours have not been forthcoming for a player with so much valuable experience.

Surely his time will come.

PETER DAVENPORT

v Republic of Ireland (March 1985)
Davenport's superb scoring record of a goal in every other game for Nottingham Forest earned him his England debut against Eire.

He came on a substitute for Mark Hateley and looked to have a chance of forcing his way into the '86 World Cup squad.

But a £570,000 transfer to Manchester United in March 1986 put paid to his hopes.

The skilful striker struggled at Old Trafford and his international chances suffered as well.

He simply couldn't settle at United and the breathtaking form he showed at Forest deserted him.

He scored just 22 goals in 92 League games and was sold on to Middlesbrough for £750,000 in 1988.

But by then the damage was done and there was no way back into the England side for him.

BRIAN MARWOOD

v Saudi Arabia (November 1988)
Marwood enjoyed one of the shortest international careers in history - just 11 minutes!

That was the length of time he was on the field after coming on as a substitute in the 79th minute of England's 1-1 draw in Riyadh.

At the time, Marwood was one of the stars of the Arsenal side which was heading for the League title.

Sadly, injuries cost him the chance of further England appearances that season and he was never able to regain the sparkling form which made him such a favourite with the Highbury fans.

But the talented winger isn't bitter about his lack of international opportunities.

He says: "It doesn't matter how long I played for, I've still got that cap and no-one can ever take it away from me."

NIGEL SPINK

v Australia (June 1983)
Spink made his only international appearance on the 1983 summer tour of Australia, when he came on as substitute for Peter Shilton in the final match of the three game series.

The big 'keeper (right) would probably have played many more times if he had been born in another era but, like Phil Parkes and Joe Corrigan before him, he found it impossible to oust Peter Shilton.

He was one of the most consistent First Division 'keepers of the 80s, and never let his Aston Villa side down during that time.

Peter Davenport in his only England game against Eire

Mel Sterland - unlucky to win just one cap

MEL STERLAND

v Saudi Arabia (November 1988)

Sterland must wonder why he was never given more of a chance at international level.

An excellent attacking full-back he is always likely to create, or even score, goals. Indeed, he's cracked more than 50 League goals during his career, an excellent record for a defender.

Right-back has proved a problem position over the years with Gary Stevens, Lee Dixon, Gary Charles and Rob Jones all being tried as both Bobby Robson and Graham Taylor searched for the answer.

But despite turning in consistently good performances for Leeds, Sterland was never in the frame for selection.

DANNY WALLACE

v Egypt (January 1986)

Wallace was discarded after just one appearance, despite scoring in the 4-0 win over Egypt.

He was in superb form for Southampton at that time and was one of the most exciting talents in the game.

His £1.2 million transfer to Manchester United in 1989 should have been the signal for him to go on and claim a regular England place.

But it didn't work out for Wallace as he failed to reproduce his Saints' form for the Old Trafford club.

He eventually drifted out of the first team picture at United and as his club career faded, so too did his hopes of an international recall.

NE CAP ONDERS

The most exclusive club in English international football is the 100 Club. Only four players have reached the magic century of 100 appearances for England, but there is another, less exclusive club. Membership is not so sought after, however. SHOOT takes a look at six of the players who've joined the ranks of the one-cap wonders in the past 10 years.

BRIAN STEIN

v France (February 1984)

Stein linked up with his Luton colleague Paul Walsh to form a new look attack against the French.

Unfortunately for Walsh and Stein, they were pitched in against a French side who went on to win the European Championship that summer.

England lost 2-0 and neither Stein nor Walsh was able to make his mark.

Stein was eventually replaced by Tony Woodcock and he never played for England again.

Playing for Luton, for years the most hated team in the country, probably didn't help his cause.

Certainly his team-mate David Preece agrees with that theory.

"A few years ago, Brian and Mick Harford were the most effective attacking partnership in the country," says Preece.

"They were tearing teams apart and should have been given the chance to do the same for England."

Brian Stein came a cropper against the French

TURNING JAPANESE

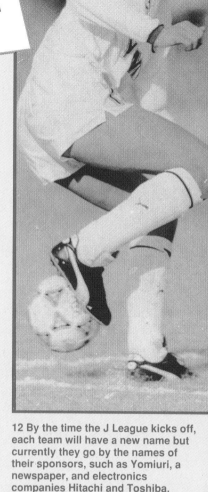

20 footballing facts about the Far East

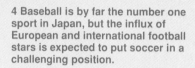

1 Japan is determined to land the first World Cup of the 21st century in the year 2002 and boosted its claims with the recruitment of England star Gary Lineker.

2 Lineker (below) signed a two-year deal worth £2.3 million with Nagoya Grampus Eight, but his capture was only the first of a mass of lucrative deals offered to foreign footballing talent.

3 The country's new ten-club J League, as it will be called, kicks off in March, 1993.

4 Baseball is by far the number one sport in Japan, but the influx of European and international football stars is expected to put soccer in a challenging position.

5 Argentines and Brazilians make up the bulk of Japanese soccer imports and, last season, the Brazilian great Zico was still active in Japan at the age of 38.

6 Bryan Robson, Chris Waddle, Ian Rush, Peter Beardsley and John Fashanu are just a few of the British players who have been linked with some of Japan's new clubs.

7 The top players in Japan currently earn between £40,000 and £140,000 a year - but those figures are sure to be magnified when the new League kicks off.

8 Japan has had a national League since 1965 and there are currently 12 teams in the First Division and 16 in the Second (they are technically non-professional and all directly attached to the companies who sponsor them). Last season's Champions were Yomiuri.

9 Lineker's club Grampus, currently called Toyota, own two stadiums, with capacities of 15,000 and 30,000. Crowds at first are expected to be no more than 5,000 but those behind the League anticipate rapid growth.

10 Toyota's average gate in recent seasons has been a little over 6,000, but the Yomiuri Giants baseball team regularly attracts sell-out crowds of 45,000.

11 Clubs are allowed three foreign players on their books, but only two are allowed to be used in any one line-up.

12 By the time the J League kicks off, each team will have a new name but currently they go by the names of their sponsors, such as Yomiuri, a newspaper, and electronics companies Hitachi and Toshiba.

13 Grampus is an English word for killer whales, while the figure eight appears in the design of the Nagoya city crest.

14 When a count was made last season, 19 foreign players who have represented their countries at national level were playing in Japan. They were made up of: 7 Brazilians, 5 Chinese, 3 Uruguayans, 2 Czechs, 1 Argentinian and 1 Thai.

15 Japan's one and only success in international football was the bronze medal its team won at the 1968 Olympics in Mexico. Striker Kunishige Kamamoto was the tournament's leading scorer, with seven goals.

Lineker's new team-mates - Grampus Eight

19 Virtually all Japanese clubs have company names and American-style cheerleaders who are office girls given the day off to encourage the team.

20 Despite its low ranking as a spectator sport, football is now the most popular participation sport in Japan.

Bryan Robson

16 Lineker will have some young colleagues at Grampus Eight. Nine high school graduates aged between 16 and 18 will account for at least half the squad. They'll be paid about £2,500 a month, plus bonuses.

17 Gary Lineker's England colleague David Platt might well end up in Japan at some stage having forged close links with Mizuno, the sportswear manufacturers with whom he signed a lucrative deal.

18 The likes of Gordon McQueen, Tony Morley, David Hodgson, John Spencer and Gary Shaw have tried their luck in Japan in the past, but when soccer was very much in its infancy.

DENIS LAW, one of the deadliest strikers of all-time, once scored six goals in a game...yet none of them counted AND HE ENDED UP ON THE LOSING SIDE!

"It was in the FA Cup in January, 1961," says Denis as he recalls one of the most sensational scoring feats in the game's history.

"I was playing for Manchester City in those days and we were drawn against Luton Town in the Fourth Round. We were 2-0 down early on in the game and then things began to happen. In an amazing burst I scored two hat-tricks to put City 6-2 ahead.

"It had been raining, but suddenly it became torrential. The sky just opened up. In fairness, the referee had no alternative but to abandon the game. You couldn't see anything because of the volume of rain and the pitch just turned into a lake."

"When the game was replayed, we lost 3-1. I had mixed feelings at the time. On the one hand I was prepared to shrug it off as just one of those things, but on the other hand I didn't enjoy us being knocked out of the Cup.

"It seemed like an injustice at the time but I don't view it the same way now. You get more realistic when you get older. I still scored six goals though - even if they didn't count."

There have been some incredible scoring stories over the years. Denis Law's is one of them, but what about George Best's?

He was the last person to score six goals in an FA Cup-tie and they all counted as Manchester United beat Northampton 8-2 in 1970.

It was a perfect performance from George, but he never did win an FA Cup winner's medal.

Nottingham Forest manager Brian Clough knows a thing or two about scoring goals. During the seven seasons between 1957 and 1963, Cloughie hit 246 League goals before injury ended his playing career.

He hammered home 193 goals for Middlesbrough and 53 for Sunderland. That's some scoring!

Ally McCoist is a Scottish League record-breaker and he is still creating new records.

When he scored for Rangers against

IT'S GOA

Ally McCoist –
a record breaker
in Scotland

Motherwell in December, 1989 it was his 128th goal in the Premier Division and beat the previous highest set by Frank McGarvey of St. Mirren and Celtic.

Mark Hateley has been stunning goalkeepers for quite a few years and he really is following in his father's footsteps.

Tony Hateley was a First Division sharp-shooter just like Mark and there was one particular occasion when his scoring skills saved the day for Aston Villa.

They were playing away to Spurs in a League match and found

Denis Law – six goals against Luton and still a loser

L MANIA!

Fantastic scoring feats that shook the game...

still unbeaten and remarkable since the tally was gained in just 39 matches.

Liverpool's Jan Molby scored his first hat-trick in the Football League in November, 1986 in a 3-1 win against Coventry - and they all came from the penalty spot..

What about a hat-trick of hat-tricks? When Manchester City hammered Huddersfield 10-1 in their Second Division clash in November 1987, Tony Adcock, Paul Stewart and David White each scored a hat-trick.

City were involved in another completely different scoring feat in 1991 when goalkeeper Andy Dibble had the ball balanced on the palm of his hand while deciding who to throw it to during his side's match at Nottingham Forest.

Forest's Gary Crosby helped him make up his mind by calmly heading the ball away from his grasp and kicking it into the net.

Just another goal that got the fans talking.

themselves three goals down within the first quarter of an hour.

Hateley pulled a goal back but Spurs were on song and extended their lead to 5-1 within a few minutes of the start of the second-half.

Villa pulled another goal back through Alan Deakin and then Tony Hateley turned on the scoring heat and hammered home another three goals in 19 minutes to give Villa a well-earned draw.

It was a Hateley super show which we can still see today thanks to son Mark.

Tony Adcock strikes for Manchester City in their 10-1 win against Huddersfield

One of the fastest goals on record came in a League match in Brazil. The referee blew his whistle, the centre-forward passed the ball to the legendary Rivelino and the international superstar blasted it straight into the net. The goal was timed at just three seconds.

It was later explained that the opposing goalkeeper had been kneeling in prayer as the referee started the game. Obviously his prayers weren't answered.

Malcolm Macdonald scored a similar goal for Newcastle in a friendly against St. Johnstone back in 1972.

The Scots 'keeper was off his line when Supermac received the ball from the kick-off and the England striker could not resist firing home at the first chance. Some friendly!

Des Walker has something of an unwanted scoring reputation . When he scored for Nottingham Forest in the last minute of a First Division game against Luton on New Year's Day 1992 it was his first ever goal in senior football.

But he still doesn't qualify for the record books because Billy Milne of Swansea played 500 League matches before scoring his first senior goal.

Milne was a full-back and it was rare indeed for defenders to score goals in the pre-war days.

You can't talk about goals without mentioning the greatest of all scorers - Dixie Dean.

Not only did he score an English record 349 goals during his career with Everton but he also hit 37 hat-tricks in his total of 379 goals in his time with Tranmere and Notts County.

He was the top scorer in the Football League in 1928 with a total of 60 at the end of that season, a figure

George Best hit six against Northampton in the FA Cup

SPOTLIGHT ON A STAR:

MO

10 things you

MO JOHNSTON and controversy have been closer companions than Hale and Pace and Fry and Laurie rolled into one. But it's not always been a laughing matter.

Fun loving, extrovert, reckless...the lot applies to the Glasgow-born playboy. There's been some sadness along the way too though.

Raids on his home, court cases, night club bust-ups and run-ins with establishment all contrived to make his life as a Celtic player in Glasgow a misery.

Yet, in typical Johnston fashion, he returned to his home town and set the tongues wagging faster and more furiously than before by signing for Rangers.

He's also turned his back on international football more than once. But, despite it all, he has no regrets.

In his autobiography, he wrote: "I have done it my way right down the line and, while I wouldn't recommend that to any young kid in the game, it is best for me."

He appears to have come through all the trials (no pun intended) and tribulations relatively unscathed - and with his bank account firmly in the black.

From Partick Thistle to Everton, via Watford, Celtic, Nantes and Rangers, Mo Johnston has lived his life 'like a candle in the wind'.

His amazing soccer talent, coupled with his built-in resistance, means the candle is still burning brightly.

Johnston broke religious barriers when he joined Rangers

JOHNSTON

never knew about Mighty Mo

1 Maurice Johnston was born in Springburn, Glasgow on April 13, 1963. As a teenager he played for the Eastercraigs youth team which also produced the likes of Willie Miller and John Wark.

2 Mo also played for the East Glasgow side, Easterhouse, alongside Pat Nevin who became a club team-mate when he joined Everton in 1991. In one of his earliest competitive matches, Mo scored all seven goals in a 7-0 win.

3 His Dad, Jimmy, played pro football for Workington and, together with Mum, Terri, was the source of his soccer inspiration. One of the family's proudest moments was when Mo was nominated Glasgow Under-12 Player of the Year.

4 Mo's best mate at school was Graham Mitchell, who persuaded him to join the Leeds United Boys Club, and the two of them played for St.Roch's secondary school in the Scottish Cup Final at Hampden Park - Mo's first appearance at the famous stadium.

5 Mo joined his first club, Partick Thistle, on £5 a week after impressing then manager Bertie Auld in a trial match against CELTIC. Just before he signed for Thistle he was offered a trial by the Parkhead club, but turned them down.

6 Mo adores dogs, and lived for his first pet Doberman 'Cairo' who he believes was poisoned by burglars who raided his home in Glasgow. He replaced 'Cairo' with two Doberman pups - and he also kept a green budgie called 'Celtic'.

Johnston joined Everton in 1991

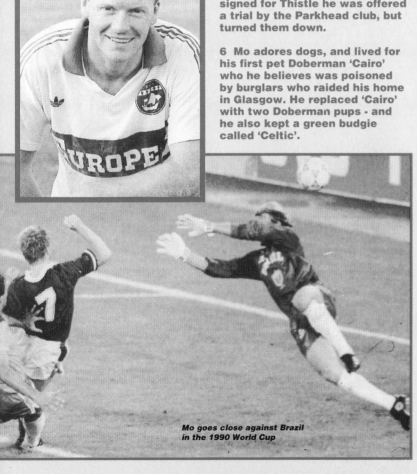

Nantes' snappy dresser

Mo goes close against Brazil in the 1990 World Cup

7 One of Mo's most embarrassing moments was turning up at his first function as a Nantes player dressed to kill in a suit and tie...while everyone else wore jeans and T-shirts. He learned his lesson and the next time he wore a pair of ripped denims.

8 In his autobiography 'MO - The Maurice Johnston Story', written while he was playing in France, he said that despite being 'hounded out' of Glasgow he would still like to go back to his home town to play and added: "I might even agree to become Rangers' first Catholic - if they paid me £1m in cash AND bought me Stirling Castle!"

9 When Mo scored a hat-trick for Watford in a 5-0 win over Wolves, he asked Molineux director Derek Dougan for the match ball but the former Northern Ireland star quipped: "We're £2m in the red and he wants the match ball."

10 After a game for Watford against Everton in 1984 (not the FA Cup Final), then boss Graham Taylor broke the news of Mo's call-up to the Scotland squad and Goodison manager Howard Kendall confessed to him: "I want to sign you for Everton."

T was an intriguing thought that Sheffield United boss Dave Bassett was wired for sound to give his comments to a local radio station during The Blades' local derby against Sheffield Wednesday last season.

Bassett being switched on is likely to set the trend for others to follow, either on radio or for live television coverage.

"I had to watch what I was saying," says Bassett. "Not that I usually use bad language but you never know."

The mind boggles. Imagine Notts County's Neil Warnock being wired up! The amount of bleeping would sound like morse code and could affect every bit of shipping around the British Isles. What about Kenny Dalglish?

wiRED FOR SOUND!

Listeners would think there had been a power cut! Ron Atkinson would take the whole thing in his stride and can out-talk Gary Newbon at any time. Danny Bergara of Stockport and Argentina's Ossie Ardiles would need subtitles if it was for television while Howard Wilkinson's chat would probably sound more like the commentary of an executioner.

It is to be hoped that the experiment would be a bit more yielding than when it was tried at a floodlit cricket match in Yorkshire's Don Valley Stadium a couple of years ago. The exciting conversation went something like this:

Commentator: "What's it like out there?"
Cricketer: "Very nice. Good crowd."
Ten minutes later
Commentator: "What's it like out there?"
Cricketer: "Yes, nice evening. Very good."

MAYBE it wouldn't be such a bad idea. More entertaining than Jimmy Hill doing his impersonation of an electric shaver or Brian Moore telling us that the Swedish referee speaks Swedish or informing us "It's Dorigo - no, it's Wallace."

Better still, why not wire up everybody, switch the whole thing to Channel Four and call it an arts programme then the swearing won't matter because nobody will be watching it anyway!

MIND you, can you think what it would be like to eavesdrop on the England bench at Wembley?

McMenemy: "It's a bit cold, Graham. I shouldn't really be sitting out here at my age."

Taylor: "Well, you can go and get the tea ready if you like, it'll be half-time soon."

McMenemy: "Alright then. How many do we need?"

Taylor: "Well there's the 11 on the pitch and this lot on the bench. Better do the ref one, he might need a sweetener."

Get the kettle on LAWRIE!

Forget the tea, boss - our lot need a drop of Carling Black Label

RUMBELOWS + SKOL CUP WINNERS
LEAGUE

CUP KINGS

Manchester United - Rumbelows Cup winners

Brian McClair skips past the challenge of Forest's Brett Williams to score United's winner and give the club their first League Cup triumph

Hibs, Hibs hooray as Keith Wright and Tommy McIntyre celebrate Skol Cup glory

Keith Wright leaves Dunfermline 'keeper Andy Rhodes helpless as he scores Hibs' second goal

THE WRITER'S CHOICE

IMAGINE yourself being named Footballer of the Year. Not just by your own supporters but by the country's top football writers, the men who have watched your performances with a critical eye all season and then say you are the best they have seen.

There can only be one player named each season and it has always been looked upon by players as something of a real honour. Today, of course there are the players' own selections but it is still the Football Writers' Association award which is the really big one.

The first man to be named as Footballer of the Year was back in 1948. If you haven't guessed, it was, of course, Stanley Matthews. Now Sir Stan, he vividly recalls that honour:

'Dreamed'

"I was playing for Blackpool at the time. I had only been there a year since transferring from Stoke in 1947. We reached the FA Cup Final but were beaten by Manchester United 4-2.

"The Football Writers had got together and decided to inaugurate this award. I never dreamed for one moment that I might be the first winner. But I was a proud man when it was announced.

"They gave it to me again in 1963 but I think they were just being kind. I was playing for Stoke and we won the Second Division Championship. I wasn't having a bad season but I was nearly 50 and I think they must have taken my age into account."

Sir Stanley was quite something. He was still playing in the First Division when he was over 50 and playing (and scoring) for England when he was in his 40s.

Matthews was not the only player to win it twice. Tom Finney was another and he speaks with pride of the day he first won the award.

"I was named Footballer of the Year in 1954 and again in 1957. I think the 1954 award was because I got to the FA Cup Final with Preston. We lost 3-2 to West Brom.

"It does fill you full of pride when someone tells you you are the best. Winning it twice was quite an honour."

Bert Trautmann, former prisoner of war who became famous as Manchester City goalkeeper, took the award in 1956. He also played in the Cup Final and that is in itself quite a tale.

In the 1955 Final, City were beaten by Newcastle, 3-1. Trautmann was in goal as he was more than 500 times. He was there again the following season and this time he received a winners' medal when City beat Birmingham 3-1.

It was all the more amazing when you consider that he was injured in a collision 15 minutes from the end of the game. An X-ray later revealed that he had broken his neck!

Bobby Moore, West Ham skipper, took the award in 1964 and then led The Hammers to FA Cup victory over Preston. The following year he led them to European Cup-Winners' Cup triumph and the year after that he led England to the ultimate - the World Cup.

Smiling

Bobby Charlton's name was on the roll of honour in 1966 and the following year it was his brother, Jack, who took the award.

"I've never been much of one for awards," said Jack. "I've got to admit though that I was smiling a lot when I got that one, especially after our kid got it the year before."

It was almost inevitable that George Best should get his name into the history

PAST WINNERS

'48 '63 STANLEY MATTHEWS

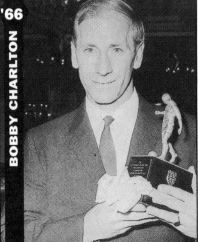

'66 BOBBY CHARLTON

'67 JACK CHARLTON

S

Gordon Strachan - tops in England and Scotland

books. He was Footballer of the Year in 1968. Manchester United were League Champions and on course for the coveted European Cup.

Gordon Banks became only the second goalkeeper to win the award when he was named in 1972. A car crash prematurely ended his career and the writers could not let the greatest goalkeeper of all time go without a suitable gesture.

The following year it was another goalkeeper who took the honours. Pat Jennings was Footballer of the Year.

Ten times in the next 18 years the award went to Liverpool players. Kenny Dalglish took it twice as did John Barnes who was the first black player to be the main man of the season.

"It's a long hard season and at the end of it it is good to win something. Getting the Footballer of the Year award has been like the icing on the cake. I appreciated it both times," said John.

There have been two breaks with tradition. In 1969 the award was jointly presented to Tony Book of Manchester City and Dave Mackay of Derby County.

City won the FA Cup and Derby took the Second Division title in such style inspired by former Spurs hero Mackay that the football scribes could not choose between the two men.

In 1989 Steve Nicol took the award on behalf of the entire Liverpool club - a gesture from the soccer writers following the Hillsborough disaster.

Thrilled

Then came another first. The first man to be named Footballer of the Year in both Scotland and England. He won the award North of the border in 1980. In 1991 he won it in England for his inspirational captaincy of Leeds United. He is, of course, Gordon Strachan.

"I was with Aberdeen when I won the Scottish award and I've got to say that I was thrilled to bits. You would think that more than ten years later things like that wouldn't mean the same. But when I won it in 1991 I felt like a kid all over again. It was great and great for the club."

CHAMPI

Richard Gough and Mark Hateley celebrat[e]
Rangers' fourth successive title

Brentford triumphed in Division Three

ONS

Leeds - top of the charts

John Pender - a winner with Burnley

Ipswich's David Linighan - tops in Two

FACTS & FUNNIES

NIGEL CLOUGH made it a proud family double when he won his first full England cap on May 23, 1989 - to add to the two caps his father Brian collected before a knee injury wrecked his playing career. But the first father and son team to play for England was George (in 1963) and George Eastham (in 1935).

OLDHAM'S SAM WYNNE (right) scored all four goals in his side's 2-2 draw with Manchester United in a Second Division clash back in October, 1923. More recently - March, 1976 - the extraordinary feat was equalled by Aston Villa defender Chris Nicholl who scored all four in a 2-2 draw with Leicester.

PRESTON are one of only two clubs to have gone through an English League season without being beaten. They did it in the League's inaugural season, 1888-89, when they went 22 games undefeated. Liverpool were also unbeaten in 28 Second Division games during the 1893-94 season.

QUEENS PARK RANGERS are one of five clubs who have won promotion from the Third Division to the First Division in successive seasons - between 1967 and 1969. Charlton did it between 1935 and 1937, Oxford 1983-85, Derby County 1985-87 and Middlesbrough 1986-88.

RALPH Banks played left-back for Bolton when they lost the 1953 'Matthews Cup Final' to Blackpool. Five years later his brother, Tom, also played in the Final of the FA Cup in the same position for the same team. The only difference being...he ended up on the winning side. The first brothers to play for England in the same match were Frank and Fred Forman in 1899.

SUBSTITUTES were first used in the Football League on August 21, 1965. Keith Peacock, who later became a manager, has the distinction of being the first ever sub when he came on for Charlton against Bolton. On the same afternoon Bobby Knox became the first sub to score in a League match when he found the net against Wrexham.

TOSTAO, the great Brazilian striker who was one of the stars of the 1970 World Cup finals, announced his retirement on exactly the same day as former England international 'keeper Gordon Banks - August 7, 1973. Ironically, both left the game because of eye injuries.

URUGUAY has the distinction of being the first country to win - and stage - the World Cup AND produce the first ever winners of the World Club Championship. Uruguay beat Argentina 4-2 in the 1930 World Cup Final while 30 years later Penarol beat Real Madrid 6-0 on aggregate to win the club title. When the second World Cup was held in 1934 in Italy, Uruguay did not bother to travel to Europe to defend their trophy.

Schumacher 'collides' with Battiston

VILLA PARK, a popular FA Cup Semi-Final venue, boasts the fourth highest record attendance in England - 76,588. Only Maine Road (84,569), Stamford Bridge (82,905) and Goodison Park (78,299) have recorded bigger attendances. In Scotland three clubs (Rangers, Queen's Park and Celtic) have all had record gates of more than 90,000.

WILLIAM HARRISON won an FA Cup winners' medal with Wolverhampton Wanderers on the same day in 1908 - April 25 - that his wife gave birth to TRIPLETS! Ironically, Wolves beat Newcastle by THREE goals to one in the Final at Crystal Palace and Harrison scored the THIRD and decisive goal.

X-RATED German goalkeeper Harald (later Toni) Schumacher has never been allowed to forget the horror tackle which almost maimed Frenchman Patrick Battiston during the 1982 World Cup in Spain. Schumacher received death threats - from Germans as well as French - but was forgiven by Battiston himself and the two have become good friends.

YORK CITY are one of six clubs who have reached the FA Cup Semi-Finals as a Third Division outfit. They did so in 1955 when they lost to Newcastle after a replay. Millwall (1937), Port Vale (1954), Norwich (1959), Crystal Palace (1976) and Plymouth (1984) have all done likewise. There have been only eight non-First Division winners of the Cup and Spurs won it as a non-League side in 1901.

ZAGALO of Brazil and Beckenbauer of West Germany are both in the record books having played for and managed World Cup winning sides. Zagalo in fact won two winners' medals as a player - in 1958 and 1962 - before guiding Brazil to their third triumph in 1970. Beckenbauer was a successful skipper in 1974 and triumphant manager in 1990.

Mario Zagalo

Nigel Clough has followed in his father's footsteps

1

CHELSEA 1 EVERTON 0

1 In which FA Cup round did the two teams meet?

2 Clive Allen, Kerry Dixon or Vinny Jones scored Chelsea's winning goal?

3 Who tripped Everton's Peter Beagrie for a penalty?

4 Who took the resultant spot-kick and what was the outcome?

5 Which Jersey-born midfielder was voted Man of the Match?

Answers on page 125

3

LIVERPOOL 2 ARSENAL 0

1 Which youngster brought down Liverpool's Ronnie Rosenthal for a penalty?

2 And who opened the scoring for The Reds from the spot-kick?

3 Liverpool's second scorer is a Republic of Ireland international. Who is he?

4 Which former Arsenal star lined up against his old team-mates?

5 David O'Leary was making his 599th, 699th or 799th appearance for The Gunners?

Compiled by Steve Pearce

TV TEA

2

MAN UTD 1 QPR 4

1 Name the England international who put Rangers ahead.

2 How many goals did Dennis Bailey score in the game?

3 Both 'keepers in the clash are foreign stars. Who were they and which countries do they represent?

4 Brian McClair, Mark Hughes or Bryan Robson grabbed United's consolation goal?

5 Is it true to say that it was United's first home defeat of the season?

4

SHEFF WED 1 LEEDS 6

1 How many goals did Lee Chapman score in the match?

2 Did Mel Sterland or Tony Dorigo score direct from a free-kick for the Elland Road club?

3 Which Wednesday striker won his side a penalty with a theatrical dive?

4 In which position did the scorer of Leeds' fifth goal, Mike Whitlow, start the game?

5 Leeds enjoyed a goal glut in another convincing away display covered live on TV. Who did they beat?

SERS

How much can you remember about the live TV coverage last season? Find out by answering these questions on four of the big games on the box during 1991-92.

LAUGH LINES

'...and to think I told all our friends to look out for you on Sportsnight'

'Just think...I'm a penniless clerk one minute and a pools' millionaire the next'

'You'd better tell him the future captain of Liverpool and England is a girl'

'I've replaced the communal bath for health reasons'

42

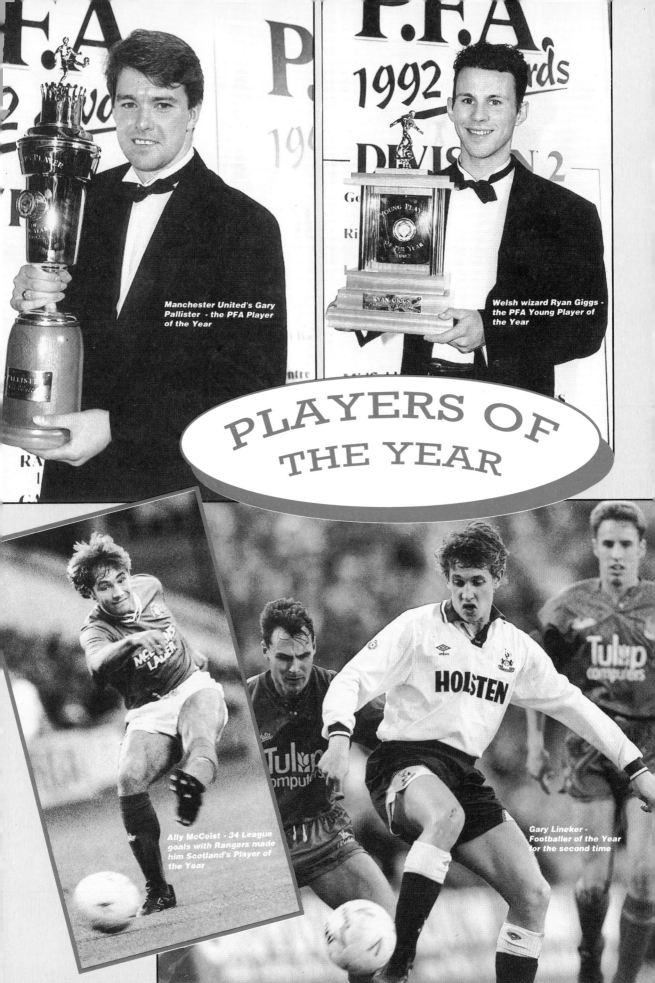

Manchester United's Gary Pallister - the PFA Player of the Year

Welsh wizard Ryan Giggs - the PFA Young Player of the Year

PLAYERS OF THE YEAR

Ally McCoist - 34 League goals with Rangers made him Scotland's Player of the Year

Gary Lineker - Footballer of the Year for the second time

CUP

Ian Rush and Michael Thomas parade the FA Cup

Rangers - Scottish Cup winners 1992

CRAZY

Michael Thomas gives Liverpool the lead against Sunderland with one of the greatest goals in FA Cup Final history

Mark Hateley strikes to give Rangers the lead in their 2-1 win over Airdrie in the Scottish Cup Final

GLENN HODDLE

Glenn Hoddle returned from his luxury lifestyle in Monaco to take charge of Second Division Swindon.

The Wiltshire club is a far cry from the jet-set life Hoddle enjoyed in France but you won't find him complaining.

And those people who believed that Hoddle was too nice for management soon found out differently.

He has a steely determination to be successful and will stick to his principles no matter what other people say.

"I insist on discipline," he says. "But you can get your point across without ranting and raving.

"I believe in good football and my team will always play the right way. Playing the long ball is the easy way and if anyone tried to tell me to play that way I'd walk away from the game."

PETER SHILTON

Peter Shilton will follow the Brian Clough management programme as he tries to emulate his former boss.

England's record cap holder enjoyed great success under Clough at Forest and says: "Brian Clough's success is a target for any new manager. I'd be more than happy to share his kind of triumphs."

Shilton has worked for some of the finest managers in English football, men like Clough, Sir Alf Ramsey, Lawrie McMenemy, Ron Greenwood and Bobby Robson.

He says: "I have been in the game 25 years and picked up things from all my managers. My targets are high - one day I want to manage England."

Firstly though, Shilton will be looking to bring some success to Home Park, Plymouth.

"I know management has a lot of casualties, but it has successes, too. That is what I intend to be.

"I aim to prove that Peter Shilton can be a great manager."

WILLIE MILLER

Willie Miller was the backbone of the Aberdeen team which achieved so much success during the 80s.

Now the former Scottish international is aiming to mastermind another golden era at Pittodrie from the manager's chair.

It's less than two years since injury forced Miller to quit playing and he admits that the move into management has come sooner than he expected.

"I've always wanted to do this job, but expected a more gradual progression," he says.

"I've been learning over the past 21 years and coaching for a few years. Running the reserves was good experience, having the scope to pick my team and make changes."

Now Miller is hoping his players show the same spirit he used to demonstrate on the pitch. "I want a committed team which entertains the fans," he says. "If we can get that we'll be up there challenging for honours."

Football management is a young man's game - or so it seems these days.

More and more players are hanging up their boots and heading straight for the manager's hot-seat.

SHOOT takes a look at some of the best known ...

Teeny

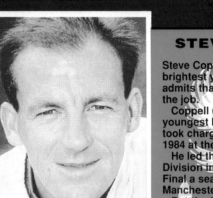

Glenn Hoddle puts the emphasis on skill in his style of management

STEVE COPPELL

Steve Coppell is one of the game's brightest young managers - but he admits that he gets no pleasure from the job.

Coppell (left) became one of the youngest bosses in the game when he took charge of Crystal Palace in June 1984 at the age of 28.

He led them to promotion to the First Division in 1989 and on to the FA Cup Final a season later, where they lost to Manchester United after a replay.

But the former United winger admits that he doesn't enjoy management. Indeed, he offered to quit after a game against Nottingham Forest last season.

He says: "If I could get another job that pays as well, I'd be off like a shot."

Peter Shilton is hoping to follow in Brian Clough's managerial footsteps

GRAEME SOUNESS

Graeme Souness has never been afraid to make tough decisions and that stood him in good stead when he was faced with the hardest choice of all: Rangers or Liverpool?

The man who made Rangers the biggest force in Scottish football, breaking down the religious barriers by signing Mo Johnston in the process, was offered the Liverpool job and had to choose between two of the game's biggest clubs.

The former Scottish international had transformed Rangers, leading them to three League Championships and three Skol Cup triumphs in his five years in charge.

But his love for Liverpool proved to be the deciding factor when it came to the crunch.

He admits: "This is the only job in Britain which could have enticed me away from Ibrox.

"It revolves around the feeling I've always had for Liverpool. I didn't think I would ever have the chance to be manager here again."

Bosses

KENNY DALGLISH

Liverpool's decision to appoint Kenny Dalglish as player-manager to succeed Joe Fagan in May 1985 shocked the football world.

Few people expected the taciturn Scot to make the transition to management, and fewer still can have expected him to do it so successfully.

In his first season in charge, The Reds became only the third club this century to complete the League and FA Cup double, with Dalglish, fittingly, scoring the goal that clinched the Championship against Chelsea at Stamford Bridge.

Further FA Cup and Championship triumphs followed before Dalglish was involved in another major shock.

If his appointment as manager was a surprise, his decision, in February 1991, to quit, sent shock-waves through the game.

Dalglish blamed the pressure of life at the top saying: "The biggest problem was the stress I was putting myself under because of my desire to become successful.

"This is the first time I've made a decision that is more favourable to myself than Liverpool FC."

But King Kenny couldn't stay away too long. Eight months later, he was back in the game as Blackburn boss.

And few people would bet against him bringing the glory days back to Ewood Park.

LENNIE LAWRENCE didn't need to be asked twice when he was offered the chance to become manager of Middlesbrough.

The man whose name had become part of Charlton Athletic folklore knew that it was time for a change and had no hesitation in heading for the North-East.

"It was in everyone's best interests that I left Charlton and I was happy to get away. Charlton needed a change as much as I did and they would have suffered if I'd stayed there."

Lawrence had been with Charlton for almost 10 years before he left for Middlesbrough so you would think that moving so far from 'home' would be a major upheaval. But Lennie simply took it in his stride.

He says: "I was coach at Lincoln for three-and-a-half years earlier in my career so I had worked outside London before which meant it wasn't a savage adjustment.

"Obviously the lifestyle is different in the North-East but it didn't take me too long to settle."

But what was it like going from a club where survival was the main aim to one who expect and demand success?

"The pressure is different and the

Lennie's Boro Boys have GREAT EXPECTATIONS

expectations are different," Lennie admits.

"Middlesbrough's average crowd is around 15,000, which is probably more than double Charlton's and that in itself brings pressure.

"Football means more to more people in the North-East than it does in South London."

Lawrence had become known as 'Houdini' for his amazing work in keeping Charlton in the First Division against all the odds for so long.

So it was no surprise that Boro enjoyed so much success last season.

And he admits: "The pressure is far worse when you are struggling at the bottom of the League than when you're pushing for promotion."

Naturally Lawrence still has fond memories of Charlton and London but he says: "I live at the other end of the country now and I love it. And there's no sign of the bloody M25!"

That's how the song goes and that certainly seems to be the way it goes for many London-born soccer stars who just can't resist a return to the capital.

Chelsea hero **PAUL ELLIOTT** could not wait to get back to the place of his birth. He began his travels away from the Smoke in 1983 when he just went up the road to join Luton.Then he went quite a bit further when he joined Italian side Pisa. Two years there and he wanted to get back to Britain. Celtic offered £650,000 in 1989 and the deal went through.

"It was good to be back in Britain, but it was still not the same as being in London. That doesn't mean that I did not enjoy being with Celtic. I have happy memories of my time there but as time went on I found that my wish to return to London was getting stronger and stronger," says Paul.

"Celtic understood how I felt and were very good although they did say that if a club came in for me the fee would have to be right. That was fair enough.

"When I heard that Chelsea were interested I was both relieved and excited and held my breath until everything was signed. There's no place like home and it meant that I could be back where I felt I belonged,

Paul **Elliott**

Paul **God**

MAYBE it's because I'm a Londoner....

near my family and my old friends. It felt good to be back in London and especially with Chelsea."

Another Paul had the same feelings about London. **PAUL GODDARD** was born in Harlington, just on the fringe of West London. He started his soccer career with Queens Park Rangers and then moved to West Ham where he had his most successful spell. Oddly enough, his next stop was Newcastle but after 61 games for The Magpies he wanted to move and then had a spell at Derby. It was Millwall who finally gave him the ticket back to London.

"I knew I would return one day, that's why I never sold my house in London. I still have it and although football may take me away from the capital, I am still a Londoner and always will be."

The same goes for an even more travelled Cockney - **RAY WILKINS**. He

was also born in Hillingdon - must be something to do with the air - and went on to make his debut for Chelsea in 1973. Almost six years later he began his travels when Manchester United bought him for £825,000. Nearly five years and quite a few England caps later he was on the road again, this time to A.C. Milan for £1.5 million. A short spell with Paris St. Germain came later and then the much publicised move to Rangers.

"I had always said that I wanted to finish my career in London and I was pleased when the opportunity to join QPR came along. West Ham were also in the frame, but I chose Rangers in the end. They are on the same side of London as I was born. I had been on the road for 12 years and like my wife and family I felt it was time to come home. Loftus Road was ideal for us."

The QPR fans will echo that.

Another QPR hero is **DENNIS BAILEY**, who scored that famous hat-trick at Old Trafford on the first day of 1992. Dennis was previously with Birmingham although born in London. A return to the capital did him a power of good.

"It's not that there was anything wrong with Birmingham, it's just that I felt so much more at home at Loftus Road. It was good to be back in London."

Former Spurs star **MARK FALCO** also tried his hand outside London after seven successful years at White Hart Lane. His first stop was Watford which can hardly be called outside London, but then he went to Scotland and joined Graeme Souness and his merry men at Ibrox. Like Wilkins, however, he wanted to go home and QPR were there to welcome him too, before he moved on to Millwall.

But what of the Londoners still playing

Ray Wilkins

Paul Furlong

Teddy Sheringham

football in the provinces?

TEDDY SHERINGHAM made no secret of the fact that he would have liked to have played for Spurs.

"I come from Highams Park which is not so very far away from White Hart Lane and I used to be a Spurs supporter. I suppose I still am really. I couldn't ask for better treatment than I have had at Nottingham Forest. Everyone has been great since I came here from Millwall and by everyone I mean from the boss, Brian Clough, who has been really good, to the fans who could not have been better.

"But many of my mates and my family are still around North London and I look forward to matches at Spurs and Arsenal which gives me the chance to see them all.

"I go to London as often as I can but I still miss it and I hope that one day I shall be able to return there, hopefully still in football."

Coventry's **PAUL FURLONG** was a van driver playing in non-League soccer. Virtually overnight he hit the jackpot and found himself playing in the First Division with Coventry.

"It all happened so fast I didn't have

time to think. I was made to feel at home at Coventry but there's still no place like London. If you talk to any Londoners playing for clubs outside the capital they'll all tell you the same."

Des Walker, Gary Charles and Stuart Pearce are three other Forest stars who hail from London.

DES WALKER is more than happy with life in Nottingham but still has a hankering after the capital.

"You can't help having a special feeling for the town you come from, but Nottingham is quite a place and I have always been happy here. That's why I wanted to stay. I'll probably go back to London when I finish playing though."

He is in good company. Paul Ince, Michael Thomas of Liverpool, Robert Rosario at Coventry, the Wallace brothers, Paul Parker, Paul McGrath, Kevin Gage, Tony Agana, Glyn Hodges, Dave Bassett, Paul Williams and many others are currently on active service away from their native London.

PAUL INCE, who gambled on the move from West Ham to Manchester United speaks for all of them.

"I was very unsettled when I first

joined Manchester United. I had an injury problem and it was touch and go whether or not I could prove that I was fit enough to get a longer contract.

"It was a great opportunity and although I still had a soft spot for West Ham I really wanted to make it with Manchester United.

"It has been very satisfying and a great experience and I hope it goes on that way. When it is all over for me here I hope to be back down the road to London. There's nowhere quite like it."

All together now - maybe it's because I'm a Londoner that I love London town ....

Perhaps a final word from the star who surprised everyone when he left London in the first place.

VINNY JONES is now happily back in London playing his heart out for Chelsea after leaving Wimbledon two years before to join Leeds and then Sheffield United.

How did he enjoy life outside London?

"I don't remember, perhaps it was just a dream."

"HAPPY BIRTHDA
HAPPY BIRTHDA

HAPPY BIRTHDA

Brian Kidd scores against Benfica in 1968.

WE ALL like to have a good day on our birthday. It's only natural. But few of us succeed in our aim as well as Brian Kidd did back in May 1968.

The 29th, to be precise. And there was young Brian, on his 19th birthday, walking out at Wembley in a Cup Final. Not just any old Cup Final, either. The European Cup Final - the first ever contested by an English club.

Celtic had won the trophy a year before, beating Inter Milan in Lisbon. This time Manchester United - given virtually a 'home' fixture - were playing Benfica.

The fairytale did have the right ending for kid Kidd. Not only did United win, 4-1, completing the dream Matt Busby had held since the days before the Munich disaster, but Kidd headed the third goal.

He had a lengthy career after that, for various clubs, but somehow nothing he did later ever matched up

Pat Jennings bowed out of international football on his 41st birthday with his 119th cap against Brazil in 1986.

TO YOU...
TO YOU..."

to that glorious birthday night.

At least three players have gained winners' medals for the FA Cup in the week of their birthday.

Big Maurice Norman, centre-half with Spurs, was born on May 8, 1934, so in both 1961 and 1962 he had extra cause to celebrate another year. Spurs won the Cup on May 6 in 1961 and did it again on May 5 a year later.

Contrasting

Jeff Astle, born on May 13, 1942, scored the only goal when West Brom beat Everton in the 1969 Final, played on May 18 that year.

And Jackie Charlton, born on May 8, 1935, won the FA Cup at the third attempt, after two losing appearances, in 1972...two days before his 37th birthday.

Two players with Wolves had contrasting Cup Final fortunes ten years apart.

Frank Taylor was the left-back in 1939, when 'Frank Buckley's Babes' finished second in the League and were beaten in the Cup Final, with one of the youngest squads ever assembled.

Taylor, who later managed Stoke City for several years, was 21 on the day after his team lost 4-1 to Portsmouth at Wembley - a shock possibly not equalled at the Stadium until Wimbledon beat Liverpool in 1988.

Ten years after poor Taylor's disaster, Wolves were back in another Final. This time little Johnny Hancocks helped them to beat Leicester, to put him in the right mood for his 30th birthday celebrations on the following day.

Derby full-back Bert Mozley appears to be the only player to make his debut for England on his birthday - rather a surprising statistic in view of the fact that over 1200 players have won caps.

Mozley played his first game on his 26th birthday, September 21, 1949, when England lost 2-0 at home to the Republic of Ireland. In his second match, England beat Northern Ireland 9-2...but he was never given another chance.

In May 1950 Bill Jones of Liverpool won his first England cap on the day after his 29th birthday, and another four days later, but they were the

Above: Double celebrations for Maurice Norman. Left: Roger Hunt.

only opportunities his country gave him. Oddly enough he was replaced at centre-half by another Liverpool player, Laurie Hughes.

Just over 16 years had passed when another Liverpool star, Roger Hunt, scored twice for his country on his 28th birthday, in the World Cup against France at Wembley.

Four years later, in another World Cup, Allan Clarke of Leeds scored the only goal of his international debut, against the Czechs.

He volunteered to take any penalties, although Johnny Giles did that job for their club, and cracked one in, no bother. It wasn't his birthday...but his wife's. And their wedding anniversary, too.

Birthdays can be sad as well as happy, of course. Pat Jennings must have had mixed feelings on June 12, 1986, his 41st birthday, when he played for Northern Ireland in a World Cup match - his 119th and last cap, then a record. Brazil put three past him.

But what a way to go!

World Cup winners USA

20 things you didn't know about women's football

GIRL

1 Women's football has been played in this country since before the turn of the century, although in 1902 the Football Association ruled that women's teams could not join the FA.

2 Preston is a hotbed of women's football and in 1884 the famous Dick Kerr XI - a factory side - was formed. On Boxing Day 1920 a game between Kerr's team and St.Helens attracted a crowd of 58,000 to Goodison Park with 10,000 fans locked out. Kerr's team disbanded in 1965.

3 Netty Honeyball was the first ever captain of the England Ladies team in 1895, but it wasn't until the 1920s that women's football became popular across Europe and the first England v France international was held.

4 After a decline in interest, the women's game sprang back to life in the 1950s when the first unofficial European Championship was held in West Berlin with England beating the hosts 4-0 in the Final. FIFA and UEFA both officially recognised the women's game in 1971.

5 The UK's first official international was held at Greenock in 1972 when England beat Scotland 3-2. A European Championship was launched in 1982 and a 'little' World Cup first staged in 1985.

6 The first official Women's World Cup tournament was held in China last November, but England failed to qualify for the finals. The tournament, which was won by the USA, attracted capacity crowds.

7 Linda Curl is Britain's most capped female footballer. She played for England 59 times between 1977 and 1990.

8 There are now a total of 380 clubs affiliated to the Women's FA in this country - a 60 per cent increase over the last two years, making women's football the fastest growing sport.

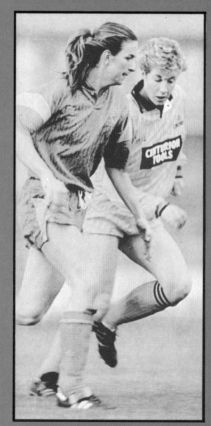
World Cup winners USA

9 In April, 1991 almost 2.5 million television viewers watched England's 5-0 defeat of Scotland - making it the most popular Channel 4 programme of the year. The game knocked 'Gazza's Soccer School' off the top slot.

10 England were drawn alongside Scotland and Iceland in Group Three of the latest European Championship. The first game took place on April 18 when England entertained Scotland.

11 Last season saw the launch of the first ever National League for women, comprising of a Premier Division and two feeder Leagues organised on a North/South basis. The League has now been expanded to three divisions of ten clubs each.

12 Britain's senior competition - prior to the launch of the National League - was the Women's FA Cup, of which Southampton were the first winners in 1971. Southampton won the trophy eight times in the first eight years of competition.

13 Although membership in this country is at its highest level - 11,000 - participation figures overseas are considerably higher. World Cup holders USA have nearly five million players, while Germany have 500,000.

14 Millwall midfielder John McGlashan became the first professional player to manage a women's team when he took control of The Lionesses last season.

LS' ALK

15 St.Helens, more renowned in Rugby League circles, made their impact on the world of soccer in 1987. The town's male team won the FA Vase and the women's side reached the Final of their FA Cup - only to lose to Doncaster Belles.

16 Thirty Football League and Vauxhall Conference clubs now boast a women's side.

17 The Belles are currently the leading women's team in Britain, having reached the Final of the WFA Cup in eight of the last nine seasons - winning four. The club also forms the nucleus of the England squad.

18 Milton Keynes were last season attempting to become the first women's club to boast their own purpose-built stadium.

19 Premier Division side Wimbledon Ladies play their home games at the club's old Plough Lane ground.

20 Tottenham Hotspur is not the only club in which White Hart Lane chief Terry Venables has a vested interest. He is also president of the Premier Division side, Maidstone Tigresses.

Doncaster Belles (white) are the leading women's team in the country

GREATEST SOCCER

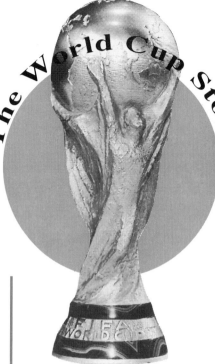

WATCH out America - here we come!

With 120 countries entered for the 1994 World Cup there will be a lot of heartache before the 24 finalists are confirmed. Matches have already started and the pattern of USA '94 is beginning to take shape even now.

Just as in the past there will be some surprises. It was all due to the work of a Frenchman, Jules Rimet, who campaigned for eight years to get the first World Cup organised in 1930. It was appropriate that the original trophy was sculptured from gold in France and called the Jules Rimet Trophy.

1930 THE FIRST TOURNAMENT was held in Uruguay with all the matches taking place in the capital, Montevideo. There were just 13 countries competing, one of them being 1994 hosts the United States. The others were Argentina, Brazil, Peru, Chile, Bolivia, Paraguay, Mexico, France, Romania, Belgium, Yugoslavia and the hosts, Uruguay.

A FRENCHMAN, Lucien Laurent, scored the very first World Cup goal as his country beat Mexico 4-1. Not surprisingly the host country made it to the Semi-Finals along with Yugoslavia, Argentina and the States. In the event, Uruguay and Argentina were left to battle it out in the Final and the hosts won 4-2, Pablo Dorado scoring the first goal for Uruguay.

There were just 18 matches in that first World Cup finals, 70 goals were scored and 434,500 people watched.

Giampiero Combi receives the trophy in 1934

1934 THE NEXT TOURNAMENT came four years later, as has become customary. This time the soccer spotlight was on Italy. An increase of entrants to 29 was whittled down to 16 and as well as the hosts, the finalists were Austria, Argentina, Belgium, Brazil, Czechoslovakia, Egypt, France, Romania, Holland, Hungary, Germany, Spain, Switzerland, Sweden and the United States.

Once again the hosts triumphed and Italy's name went on the trophy as 1934 winners. With the competition run on a knockout basis there were just 17 matches watched by 395,000 people.

1938 FOR THE first time, the host country, France, did not win it. In fact, they were knocked out in the Second Round by the eventual winners who also became the first country to win the World Cup on foreign soil and the first to retain it. Yes, it was Italy who stole the show, beating Hungary 4-2 in front of 45,000 people in Paris. This

time there were 18 matches and 84 goals. Attendances were up as well with 483,000 spectators.

World War Two disrupted the competition for the next 12 years.

1950 THE WORLD CUP roared back in 1950 although only 13 nations took part. The hosts were Brazil and for the first time the British countries took part, although it was left to England to carry the flag. The other finalists were Yugoslavia, Switzerland, Spain, Italy, Sweden, Mexico, Chile, Paraguay, Bolivia, Uruguay and, once again the United States.

WHAT A SHOCK there was in store for England though. They won their first match, 2-0 against Chile. But the second match was a disaster, losing 1-0 to the United States. The next game also ended in demoralising

Italy - winners again in 1938

defeat, Spain winning 1-0.

The Final in Rio was watched by 193,850 people, most of them cheering on Brazil, who were pipped 2-1 on the day by Uruguay. That attendance was a record which still stands. The tournament's 22 games produced 84 goals and topped a million spectators for the first time - 1,337,000 to be exact.

1954 IT WAS BACK to Europe for the 1954 finals, Switzerland the hosts. For the first time the tournament was televised. From Britain, England were competing again and Scotland made their debut in the finals. The hosts were there, of course, and the trophy holders. They were joined by Austria, Belgium, Czechoslovakia, France, Hungary, Italy, Turkey, Yugoslavia, West Germany, Brazil, Mexico and Korea. For the first time the United States were missing.

A record 140 goals were scored in the 26 matches. England won their group but were defeated 4-2 by Uruguay in the Quarter-Finals. Scotland had a nightmare. They lost their first match 1-0 against Austria but there was worse to come as Uruguay hammered them 7-0.

West Germany beat Hungary 3-2 in a classic Final in front of 60,000 spectators and many, many more watching on television. Overall attendance figure was 943,000.

SHOW ON EARTH

A lap of honour for the 1958 Brazilians

Brazilian captain Mauro holds aloft the 1962 Jules Rimet trophy

1962 THE SEVENTH tournament saw 16 nations line up in Chile. The world held its breath as all eyes turned to see what Pele could do this time around. Unfortunately he was injured early on in the tournament but the strong Brazilians were still a match for anyone. England were the only British side taking part and despite an early defeat by Hungary, they went on to defeat Argentina 3-1 and draw with Bulgaria 0-0, good enough to reach the Quarter-Finals, where Brazil proved to be just a bit too strong and won 3-1. In the England squad were two particularly notable names - Jimmy Greaves and Bobby Charlton.

Brazil were unstoppable and gave Czechoslovakia the run around in the Final, winning 3-1 in style.

1966 ALF RAMSEY - before his knighthood - was in charge of England's hopes.

1958 EUROPE STAGED the finals again four years later. This time it was in Sweden. England, Scotland, Wales and Northern Ireland were all there, along with 12 others. But there was something else - or rather someone else. In 1958, there was a 17-year-old international player who was about to turn the course of soccer history - yes, Pele.

Once again Scotland finished at the bottom of their group, England finished second in theirs but needed to finish first to qualify. They did not lose a game, but they did not win one either. Wales had the same problem and finished third, but while England lost their play-off match against USSR, Wales beat Hungary in their play-off and were in the Quarter-Finals. Northern Ireland also had to go through a play-off game and stunned everyone by beating a very strong Czechoslovakia.

In the Quarter-Finals the Irishmen were well beaten by France, but plucky Wales put up a tremendous fight before going down 1-0 to Brazil. The scorer - yes, it had to be Pele. He went a stage further in the Semi-Finals and scored a hat-trick in Brazil's 5-2 win over France.

An intriguing Final saw the hosts Sweden pitched against Brazil. Sweden played well but the watching 49,737 and the millions of TV viewers were hypnotised by the sheer magic of the Brazilian game. The South Americans won 5-2 with such finesse as had never been seen before. Young Pele scored twice and was the toast of world soccer.

England's first game was a bit of a damp squib. The result was a 0-0 draw against Uruguay. Then Bobby Charlton scored an amazing goal against Mexico. England were on their way. None of the other Home nations had qualified so England had to do well. Brazil were hungry for a third win, as were Italy and Uruguay. Brazil were kicked off the park and never allowed to show their true style. Pele was bruised and battered once again as the result became more important than the game.

The epic Final has been relived countless times but, of course, it was England's finest two hours with an extra-time triumph over West Germany 4-2. Don't let anyone fool you - they deserved it.

The name of Banks, Cohen, Wilson, Stiles, Jack Charlton, Moore, Ball, Peters, Bobby Charlton, Hurst and Hunt will live forever as the men who won the World Cup for England in 1966.

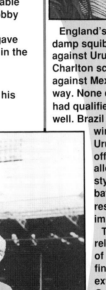

Geoff Hurst was England's hat-trick hero

The World Cup Story

Franz Beckenbauer holds aloft the '74 World Cup

1970 IT WAS LEFT to England to fly the flag again four years later when, as World Champions, they automatically qualified for the 1970 tournament in Mexico. In their group England beat Romania and Czechoslovakia but lost 1-0 to Brazil. They made it to the Quarter-Finals though where things were going well until concentration fell apart near the end. England were leading West Germany 2-0 and looking very comfortable - too comfortable. West Germany bounced back, grabbed two late goals and then a winner in extra-time.

Italy beat West Germany in the Semi-Finals and then had to show what they could do in the Final against Brazil. Someone was going to win the World Cup for a third time. Brazil were devastating. Pele was in fantastic form and nobody was going to stop them making the Jules Rimet Trophy their own by grabbing that third triumph. The Italians were left in their wake in a superb display in the Final which the South Americans won 4-1.

1974 WEST GERMANY were hosts in 1974 and this time it was left to Scotland to represent Britain, England and the others having failed to qualify. There were some unusual names in the finals list, several countries qualifying for the first time - East Germany was one but there was also Haiti, Zaire and Australia.

Scotland recorded their first World Cup finals win, beating Zaire 2-0, but they did not get past the First Round. Those that did were split into groups again and the winners of each group became finalists. It was Holland and West Germany. The drama came almost straight from the kick-off. The Dutch launched the first attack, Johan Cruyff was felled in the area and Holland took an early lead from the penalty spot. Their celebrations lasted only 24 minutes though

because West Germany stormed back and were themselves given a penalty and then went ahead just before half-time. The score remained at 2-1 and the hosts stamped their name on the new trophy but the world applauded Holland and Cruyff.

1978 THE DUTCH proved that it was no fluke when they reached the Final of the 1978 World Cup, this time held in Argentina. Once again only Scotland made it for Britain and they were brimming with confidence when they flew from these shores. However, they were shamed when they the lost their first match 3-1 to Peru. Then they could only draw 1-1 with Iran and the cold truth was that they were out. There was still one game to play though and Scottish pride made them give it their best shot. Steered by Archie Gemmill (left) they beat the mighty Holland 3-2.

Meanwhile, the hosts were playing some good football. In

Simply the best - Brazil 1970

the Second Round they had to finish top of their group to reach the Final and by the sort of mathematics that can sometimes reduce soccer to a computer game, Argentina had to win their last game against Peru by four goals to reach the Final. They went two better, winning 6-0.

Holland put up a great fight in the Final but Argentina were not going to give up now, especially in front of their fiercely partizan crowd. It was a closely contested game but Argentina were worthy winners at 3-1.

ON EARTH

1982 INTO 1982 and all eyes were on Spain. There was an increase in the number of finalists, with 24 being split into six groups. England were there, Scotland were there and Northern Ireland were there - with record-breaking Norman Whiteside, who at 17 years and 42 days took Pele's title as the youngest ever World Cup player.

England made a great start, winning all three matches against France, Czechoslovakia and Kuwait. They easily won their group. Scotland beat New Zealand, drew with USSR but were well beaten by Brazil. They didn't get through. It was Northern Ireland who provided the shocks though. They drew with Yugoslavia and then Honduras but pulled out all the stops to beat Spain on their own soil and win their group.

Phase two saw England draw their two group matches, not good enough to reach the Semi-Finals. Northern Ireland drew and then lost and they too caught the plane home, but to a great reception. The Final in Madrid was between Italy and West Germany. The Germans were disappointing. Italy took full advantage, played some exciting soccer and became the first Europeans to win the World Cup three times. Attendances at the matches topped 1,766,277. The competition had come a long way in 50 years.

1986 FOUR YEARS later everyone should have been gathering in Colombia but the proposed hosts withdrew late in the day and the honour went to Mexico, the first country to stage the World Cup finals twice. England were there, Scotland were there and Northern Ireland did it again. This time the Irish spirit was not quite enough to see them through their group. Scotland were once again disappointing and finished bottom of their group. England were slow starters but gradually picked up momentum and qualified for the next round by finishing second in their group which

was amazingly won by Morocco.

A solid 3-0 success over Paraguay saw England into the Quarter-Finals, where they tended to stop and stare as Maradona was given the freedom of the park to both run with the ball and give a demonstration of basketball. The Argentinians won 2-1 and even Maradona later admitted that his first goal was a deliberate handball.

It was another stepping stone to the Final for Argentina though, and there they met West Germany who tried to play football and looked more than capable of winning but eventually lost 3-2. Viewing figures reached 12.8 billion while 2,285,498 were at the matches. Consolation for England was that Gary Lineker was the tournament's top scorer.

1990 AND SO to Italia '90. The host country were red hot favourites to win again. But there were surprises all the way. England had qualified but had already been written off by the 'experts'. Scotland were there and, so too, for the

first time, were the Republic of Ireland, who were drawn in the same group as England.

The tournament's opening match set the pattern. Champions Argentina played against unknown Cameroon. Sensationally the Africans won 1-0 but there were two sendings-off and a great deal of battering and amateur dramatics. There was more to come. Scotland approached their opening game against Costa Rica with obvious confidence. Unbelievably their tale of World Cup woe continued as they lost 1-0. They later beat Sweden but lost to Brazil which meant the early plane home once again. England and Eire met in an intriguing opening group game, the wits of Messrs Robson and Charlton pitted against each other. It was a draw. They both went on to qualify for the next round.

England beat Belgium, and Eire beat Romania on penalties to reach the Quarter-Finals. In one of the best matches of the competition England then beat Cameroon 3-2 while Ireland went out, losing 1-0 to hosts Italy.

The Irish made a lot of friends but the reigning Champions were losing more and more. Argentina were putting more emphasis on displays of petulance than on soccer. They won on penalties to reach the Semi-Finals and then again on penalties to reach the Final.

West Germany also won on penalties in their Semi-Final, where their victims were England. Gazza cried, Robson was disappointed but at home they were getting a standing ovation.

The Final was a bad-tempered let-down. Two Argentinians, Gustavo Dezotti and Pedro Monzon, became the first ever players to be sent-off in the Final and West Germany just about earned their 1-0 victory.

1994 AND NOW we are on the trail to the USA and World Cup '94.

America will come alive nearer the time and in true tradition we shall see the game presented at a level somewhere between Disneyland and the Superbowl. The home crowds will be cheering on their own men - "all the way with USA" even if they will be watching scoreboards to see if a goal has been scored.

West Germany's Lothar Matthaus celebrates their 1990 triumph

Norman Whiteside - the youngest player ever to play in the World Cup finals

Maradona gives Argentina a helping hand

ACTION

SKY BLUE: Coventry's Paul Furlong wins this aerial duel with Chelsea's Graeme Le Saux

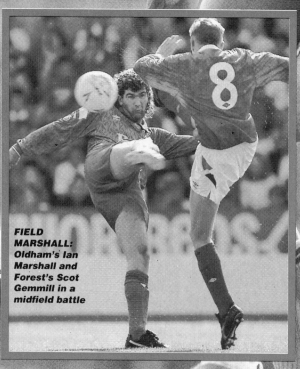

FIELD MARSHALL: Oldham's Ian Marshall and Forest's Scot Gemmill in a midfield battle

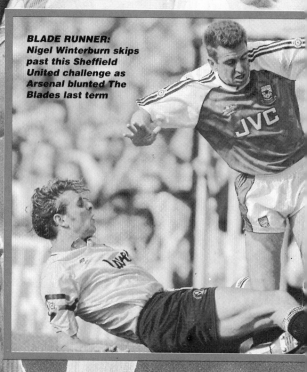

BLADE RUNNER: Nigel Winterburn skips past this Sheffield United challenge as Arsenal blunted The Blades last term

'93

TOP MARK: Rangers striker Mark Hateley comes out on top in this clash with Dunfermline's Davie Moyes

FIRST CLASS

Shearer and Merson join England's debut day dazzlers

WHEN it comes to dashing debutants, there are few better than Alan Shearer.

Whatever the level, whatever the opposition, the Geordie genius always comes up trumps.

During a brief, yet, glittering career so far he has banged in goals on his first appearance for the following:-

* Wallsend Boys Club;
* Cranlington Juniors;
* Southampton youth, reserves and first team;
* England Under-19s, 21s and national side.

He served notice of his massive potential when he launched his professional career with a hat-trick as an 18-year-old unknown against Arsenal.

And it's been goals all the way ever since for the lad who wrote his name into the record books with his first full international goal against France last season.

He joined such illustrious names as Jimmy Greaves, Bobby Charlton, Roger Hunt, Francis Lee, Allan Clarke and, more recently, Glenn Hoddle and Steve Bull.

Superstardom

His debut day strike against the French elevated him to overnight superstardom.

He says: "Before the start of last season I was just Alan Shearer, professional footballer. One goal for England and suddenly I was Alan Shearer, public property.

"But I can live with all that. Much of my career has been a dream come true. To score on my England debut has been the highlight though."

Praise poured in from all quarters and England number two Lawrie McMenemy was at the head of the queue of admirers.

"Alan is the cool, quiet, silent type. You can see goals in his eyes. He loves them," enthused Big Mac. "And all his success won't go to his head. He is a mature lad who handles publicity well."

'Maturity' was perhaps not a word which sprang to mind to describe Arsenal's Paul Merson a couple of years ago, but he's grown up now and an international star of the future.

And he joined the happy band of debut day scorers when he notched in his first full appearance for the national side in last season's 2-2 draw in Czechoslovakia.

DEBUT DAY DELIGHT

Your check on those England players who have scored on their first outing :-

YEAR	PLAYER OPPONENTS	SCORE/NO.OF GOALS
1946:	Tom Finney v Northern Ireland	7-2/One
	Wilf Mannion v Northern Ireland	7-2/Three
	Robert Langton v Northern Ireland	7-2/One
1947:	Stan Mortensen v Portugal	10-0/Four
1948:	Jackie Milburn v Northern Ireland	6-2/One
	John Rowley v Switzerland	6-0/One
	John Haines v Switzerland	6-0/Two
	John Hancocks v Switzerland	6-0/Two
1949:	John Morris v Norway	4-1/One
	Jack Froggatt v Northern Ireland	9-2/One
1950:	John Lee v Northern Ireland	4-1/One
	Nat Lofthouse v Yugoslavia	2-2/Two
1951:	Harold Hassall v Scotland	2-3/One
	Bill Nicholson v Portugal	5-2/One
1953:	Dennis Wilshaw v Wales	4-1/Two
1954:	John Nicholls v Scotland	4-2/One
	Don Revie v Northern Ireland	2-0/One
	Johnny Haynes v Northern Ireland	2-0/One
1955:	Geoffrey Bradford v Denmark	4-1/One
	Peter Atyeo v Spain	4-1/One
1956:	Colin Grainger v Brazil	4-2/Two
	Gordon Astall v Finland	5-1/One
	John Brooks v Wales	3-1/One
1957:	Derek Kevan v Scotland	2-1/One
	Alan A'Court v Northern Ireland	2-3/One
	Bobby Robson v France	4-0/Two
1958:	Bobby Charlton v Scotland	4-0/One

YEAR	PLAYER OPPONENTS	SCORE/NO.OF GOALS
1959:	Jimmy Greaves v Peru	1-4/One
	Joe Baker v Northern Ireland	2-1/One
	Ray Parry v Northern Ireland	2-1/One
1960:	Bobby Smith v Northern Ireland	5-2/One
1961:	Gerry Hitchins v Mexico	8-0/One
	Ray Pointer v Luxembourg	4-1/One
1962:	Roger Hunt v Austria	3-1/One
	Mike O'Grady v Northern Ireland	3-1/Two
1963:	Tony Kay v Switzerland	8-1/One
1964:	Fred Pickering v USA	10-0/Three
	Frank Wignall v Wales	2-1/One
1969:	Francis Lee v France	5-0/One
1970:	Allan Clarke v Czechoslovakia	1-0/One
1971:	Chris Lawler v Malta	5-0/One
1975:	David Johnson v Wales	2-2/Two
1976:	Ray Kennedy v Wales	2-1/One
	Peter Taylor v Wales	2-1/One
1979:	Glenn Hoddle v Bulgaria	2-0/One
1982:	Paul Goddard v Iceland	1-1/One
	Sammy Lee v Greece	3-0/One
	Mark Chamberlain v Luxembourg	9-0/One
1986:	Danny Wallace v Egypt	4-0/One
1989:	Steve Bull v Scotland	2-0/One
1991:	Dennis Wise v Turkey	1-0/One
1992:	Alan Shearer v France	2-0/One

* NOTE: Only three players have scored three or more goals on their England debut since the War: Wilf Mannion, Stan Mortensen and Fred Pickering.

EOIN JESS

ABERDEEN
A FC
1903
FOOTBALL CLUB

Teddy Sheringham
★ ★ ★ ★ ★ ★ ★ ★ ★ ★ ★ ★ ★ ★ ★ ★ ★
NOTTINGHAM FOREST

IAN'S MERSEY GOAL RUSH

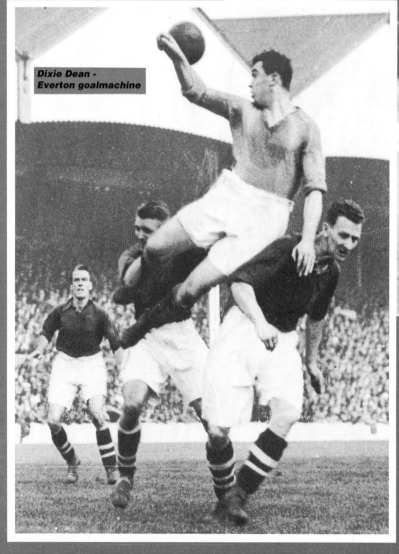

ONE of the most remarkable scoring records of recent times is that achieved by Ian Rush of Liverpool in Merseyside derby matches against the old foes from across Stanley Park, Everton.

Rush has scored the impressive total of 24 goals in 29 appearances, three of them as substitute. That's easily a Merseyside record, beating former Everton great Dixie Dean's old figure of 18 in 17 matches back in the 1920s and 30s.

But should the Rush total be recognised as a record after all...or not? We think that the question depends on what you mean by a 'first-class' match. And that in turn poses another problem. If we are going to have first-class matches and 'other' matches who is going to decide which is which?

Strange

Rush has scored 12 Football League goals against Everton, in 17 matches. He has notched five FA Cup goals, in five games, one in three League Cup appearances, one in two Charity Shield fixtures, and five in two games in a strange competition called the ScreenSport Super Cup.

Remember that one? It was brought in as a TV venture to help fill the gap when English clubs were out of Europe as a result of the Heysel disaster.

Liverpool beat Southampton in 1985 to qualify for the Final, but because of fixture congestion that had to be held over until the following year, when Liverpool smashed Everton 3-1 and 4-1. After that, the trophy died an apathetic death.

Now, are matches in that particular competition worthy of being called first-

Dixie Dean - Everton goalmachine

class? Obviously no Liverpool-Everton game is ever taken less than seriously, and Rush no doubt worked as hard for his goals in those games as he did for any of the others he has obtained.

But is it right that a tournament restricted to four clubs, by invitation only, as a TV bonanza, should merit inclusion in club records?

The same applies to the Charity Shield. Usually that is between League Champions and FA Cup winners, but it is not always so. Should achievements in that two-club, one-off contest be counted in records?

Going back to Merseyside, there is no record of Dean's achievements in

'other' matches against Liverpool. We know that he scored 17 goals in 16 First Division matches against them, including two hat-tricks, plus one goal in the only FA Cup-tie between them during his career.

There was no League Cup in those days, certainly no ScreenSport, no Texaco Cup or Simod Cup or Full Members Cup or Freight Rover Trophy or any other of the competitions set up to keep turnstiles clicking.

But it is possible that Dean played (and scored) against Liverpool in two other tournaments - the Lancashire Cup and the Liverpool Senior Cup, which were rather more important in Dixie's day than they are now.

We'll never know the exact figures. But we feel that there should be some ruling authority able to sort matters like this out.

There doesn't seem to be this problem in other sports. Cricket has its Test and County Cricket Board to sort out international problems, and the MCC to handle other disputes. Golf? The Royal and Ancient at St. Andrew's is the sole ruling authority. Motor racing? FISA. Wimbledon? That's the big gun in tennis. And so on, and so on.

Can somebody, somewhere, take responsibility for soccer's facts, figures and feats? It's all so confusing at present.

Calyp

Yorke so nearly reached the 1990 World Cup finals with Trinidad

DWIGHT YORKE is now reaping the benefits of a three-year fight against the elements...and his emotions.

More accustomed to the Caribbean sunshine, Trinidad-born Dwight found the frost and fog of a typical winter's morning in England about as appealing as a Wimbledon v Sheffield United clash in front of 4,000 fans at Selhurst Park.

In fact the warmest he's been since his arrival at Villa Park in 1989 was when he discovered how to work Ron Atkinson's sun bed!

The hard pitches were a problem for the young Yorke too and he says: "When I arrived I'd never really experienced anything like that first cold spell before. But it's something I've got used to over the last three years."

Dwight also found it difficult when, as a 17-year-old, he was living in digs, 4,000 miles from his home and his family.

"My first six months here were the worst," he explains. "But I've got my own house now, I've made lots of good friends and I've adjusted to a new way of life. I feel completely comfortable."

Over the last year, Dwight gives a lot of the credit for his rapid development to Villa boss Atkinson and his experienced colleague Cyrille Regis.

"Cyrille's been very helpful, as he is with all the younger players," says Dwight. "He always finds the time to have a chat with us, and he reminds us of the need to behave the right way even when we're not playing."

Atkinson has been delighted with Yorke's progress and says: "Dwight makes things happen when the ball's at his feet, but the thing that has surprised me is how good he is in the air. His greatest asset, however, has been his willingness to learn."

By his own admission Yorke admits he is still learning and, while Graham Taylor continues to sing the praises of the young player he discovered, he reckons: "I think there's a lot more to come from Dwight Yorke."

so kid

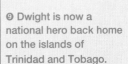

Cyrille Regis has been a great help to Yorke

TEN THINGS YOU NEVER KNEW ABOUT THE CALYPSO KID

❶ He hails from Trinidad and Tobago in the West Indies and was born on March 3, 1971

 ❷ He was spotted playing in the Caribbean by England boss Graham Taylor when he was in charge at Villa.

❸ Dwight played football for Trinidad at all levels, but he also considered a career as a cricketer.

 ❹ When he first came to England he struggled to come to terms with the cold weather and used to wear a hat and gloves during training.

❺ Former Manchester United boss Tommy Docherty once said of Yorke 'if he's a First Division footballer, I'm Mao-Tse Tung'.

 ❻ Dwight played World Cup football before making a name for himself in the English First Division.

❼ He is a great admirer of team-mate Cyrille Regis who took him under his wing when the two came together at Villa.

 ❽ He signed for Villa in December, 1981 and within 18 months had played under three different managers - Graham Taylor, Jozef Venglos and Ron Atkinson.

❾ Dwight is now a national hero back home on the islands of Trinidad and Tobago.

 ❿ He is no giant when it comes to height (he's only 5ft 10ins) but Dwight possesses natural spring which makes him a constant danger in the air.

The Dragon

Gary Speed is a fine prospect

FOR so long Wales have been the nearly men of international football. So near yet so far has been the heart-breaking story on numerous occasions.

Despite their side boasting the likes of Rush, Hughes, Saunders, Southall and Ratcliffe, Wales have failed to qualify for a major Championship since the 1958 World Cup finals.

They were twice denied a place in the World Cup finals - in 1978 and 86 - by controversial penalty incidents in games against Scotland.

And they were narrowly pipped to a place in last summer's European Championship finals by Germany.

"That was a major disappointment," admits manager Terry Yorath. "We played well in the qualifiers but Germany were always favourites."

But all this disappointment could soon be swept aside. Wales have an excellent crop of young players coming through and Yorath is hopeful that

RYAN GIGGS is the best known of Wales' young starlets but there are several others coming through the ranks who Yorath is equally impressed with.

Naturally though, Giggs is the player everybody is talking about.

He became the youngest ever Welsh international when he made his debut against Germany last November, aged just 17 years and 349 days.

That beat John Charles' 40-year-old record by 87 days to earn Giggs a place in the history books.

And Yorath is well aware that in the young Manchester United star, he has a player of breathtaking talent at his disposal.

"If he continues his progression

World-beater Giggs

and gets a bit of luck with injuries and such like he will be one of Wales' greatest ever internationals," enthuses Yorath.

"He has electrifying pace, is good on the ball and has an excellent tem-

perament. There's nothing negative about him and that's very refreshing."

But Giggs isn't the only young star who Yorath has high hopes for.

"Luton's Mark Pembridge is another who could be an international for the next ten years," says Terry. "He's a very strong, competitive player - just the type you want around. And

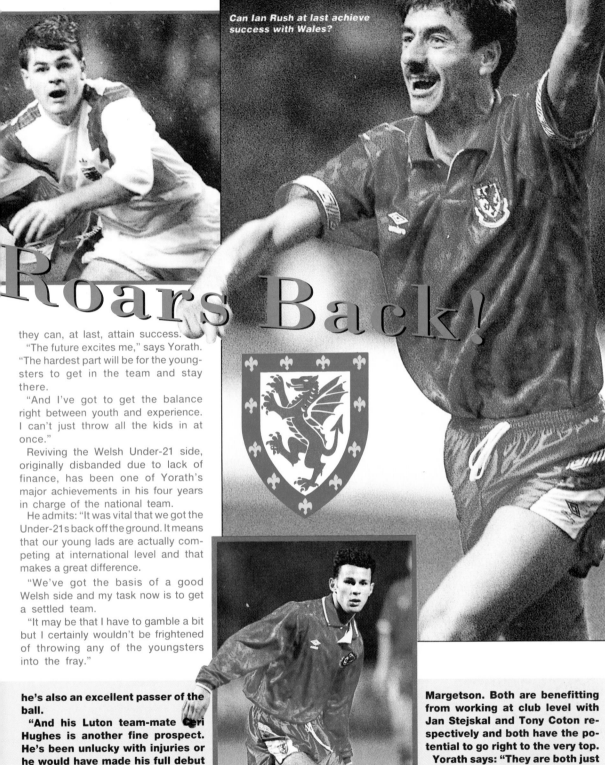

Can Ian Rush at last achieve success with Wales?

Roars Back!

they can, at last, attain success.

"The future excites me," says Yorath. "The hardest part will be for the youngsters to get in the team and stay there.

"And I've got to get the balance right between youth and experience. I can't just throw all the kids in at once."

Reviving the Welsh Under-21 side, originally disbanded due to lack of finance, has been one of Yorath's major achievements in his four years in charge of the national team.

He admits: "It was vital that we got the Under-21s back off the ground. It means that our young lads are actually competing at international level and that makes a great difference.

"We've got the basis of a good Welsh side and my task now is to get a settled team.

"It may be that I have to gamble a bit but I certainly wouldn't be frightened of throwing any of the youngsters into the fray."

he's also an excellent passer of the ball.

"And his Luton team-mate Ceri Hughes is another fine prospect. He's been unlucky with injuries or he would have made his full debut sooner."

Gary Speed at Leeds, Andrew Melville at Oxford and Bristol City's Robbie Edwards are others about whom Yorath enthuses.

And he also has two excellent young keepers waiting in the wings to take over from the outstanding Neville Southall.

They are Tony Roberts at QPR and Manchester City's Martin Margetson. Both are benefitting from working at club level with Jan Stejskal and Tony Coton respectively and both have the potential to go right to the very top.

Yorath says: "They are both just waiting for Neville to hang up his gloves. I would have no worries about playing either of them in a full international.

"Wales have always had good goalkeepers but these two are just below Neville. They really are that good."

All in all the future looks rosy for Wales. All they need now is a little bit of luck.

LIVE soccer on Sky Sport has really taken off during the last season or so. Sky cameras have taken us all over Britain and even into Europe and around the soccer globe to capture the very best in football.

It all seems so easy. The presenters just pop along, talk to a few stars, watch a game and go home. But of course, it's not quite as simple as that as Shoot found out when we went behind the scenes of a live and exclusive FA Cup Quarter-Final tie...Chelsea v Sunderland

SKY'S

THE wagons roll into the Stamford Bridge ground at about nine o'clock in the morning. They have just travelled down from Yorkshire where they were attending a rugby match the day before.

When the transport arrives and is parked the cables have already been laid - all three kilometres of them! They have to go to 20 different cameras and sound sources. That is the job of PETER HORTON, the Production Manager in charge of the technicians.

The panel - Ron Atkinson and Vinny Jones with Richard Keys

COMMENTATOR MARTIN TYLER arrives about four hours before the game. He has already been working hard all day at his Surrey home studying all the very latest information on the teams, the players, past results, the referee - anything that might be of interest to the viewer.

Martin has been a television commentator for 17 years and loves every minute of it. "It's a wonderful job. I wouldn't swop it for anything," he says. Chelsea's suspended star VINNY JONES joins him for a chat.

RICHARD KEYS is the face of soccer on Sky Sport. Nationally known as a presenter of TV-AM he is enjoying life much more these days by spending all his time with his favourite sport.

"I am obsessed by football," he says. "I always have been. It is a great joy to be able to work and talk football with people like Andy Gray and Ron Atkinson who are regulars on our coverage. I must have one of the best jobs in the world."

Richard has also been studying for the game. He knows that if there are any delays or problems he will have to keep things going until the game continues.

THE LIMIT

The action – Clive Allen gives Chelsea the lead against Sunderland

The voice – Martin Tyler

THE STADIUM fills up and there is a wall of sound around the ground as a noisy 5,000 Sunderland fans compete with almost 30,000 Londoners. It's a draw on the terraces. Sky Soccer supremo Vic Wakeling surveys the scene.

It's 7pm and we are going live from Stamford Bridge with 45 minutes before kick-off. Time to soak in the atmosphere, get the predictions and point out the facts. Behind the scenes the rest of the crew are growing in excitement. Amazingly as they push buttons and turn dials

they still have time to enjoy the game.

REFEREE TERRY HOLBROOK blows his whistle and the game gets under way. Martin Tyler gets to work, Richard Keys watches the match and the crew push buttons even more excitedly.

Chelsea press. A corner is given. It's a good talking point because the cameras show that it was a Chelsea player who last touched the ball. The corner is taken, legs and heads fly, the ball ricochets and Clive Allen turns it into the net.

Even as they push the buttons, the behind-the-scenes crew leap to their feet. Outside, 30,000 Londoners do the same. In the homes a couple of million people are celebrating.

CONTINUED OVERLEAF

SKY'S THE LIMIT

HALF-TIME and statistician Dave Hamilton updates his facts and figures. Roving interviewer Nick Collins stands by the tunnel with his microphone. Richard, Ron and Andy have a chat in the studio. Vinny joins them.

THE SECOND-HALF continues as exciting as the first. Sunderland work hard to grab an equaliser. Chelsea defend well. Time is running out. The Roker faithful roar on their men. Then it happens. Just eight minutes left and John Byrne heads home an equaliser. The fans erupt. The technicians leap in the air again. Every goal is worth a celebration when you are live on Sky Sport.

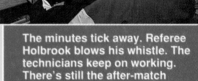

The minutes tick away. Referee Holbrook blows his whistle. The technicians keep on working. There's still the after-match interviews and comments to do.

AT LAST the programme is over and everyone slumps into their seats for a few minutes. Then it's time to pack up and go home. It will be after midnight when the wagons roll out again.

"How far is it to Sunderland?" Someone asks. Everyone starts to talk about it - they know they will be there for the replay. That's what Sky Sport is all about.

The equaliser – John Byrne levels things up for the Roker men

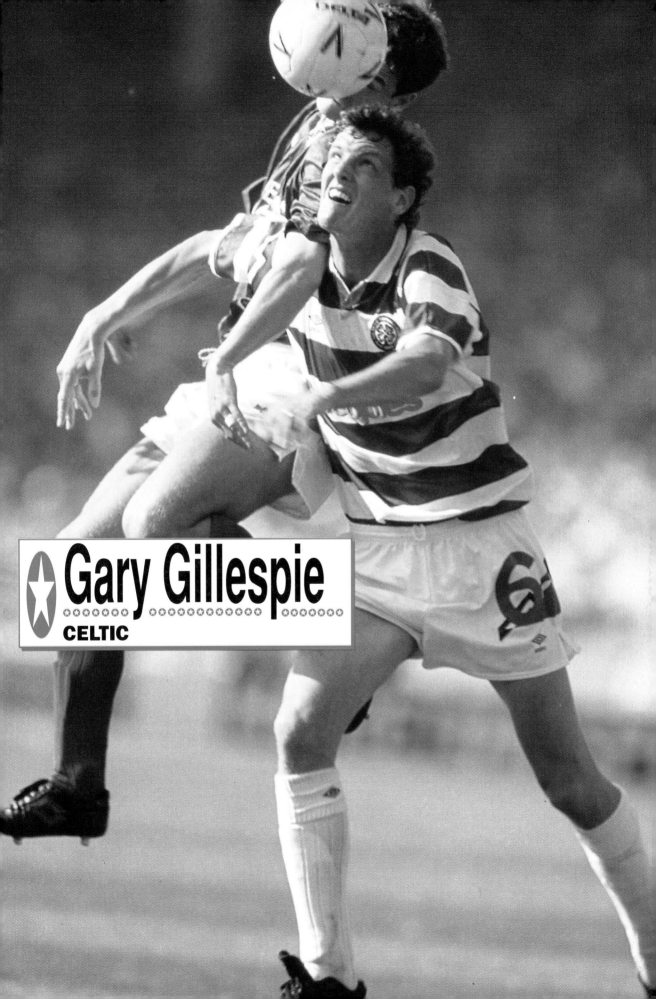

Gary Gillespie
★★★★★ ★★★★★★★★★★ ★★★★★★
CELTIC

LAUGH LINES

'I could have chosen a simple job...lawyer, brain surgeon, Prime Minister...but no I had to be a football club manager'

'You've got a mention in the paper, dear, just below the 'printed by'

'I never touched him, ref'

'Don't get changed, lads, I think the game's off'

'I think the local soccer hoolies are trying to impress us, sarge'

It's been goals all the way for Barnet

going to change, whether we're playing Chesham at home or Manchester United away."

Within weeks of bursting onto the Football League scene, Barry's Barnet proved his point. They charged to the top of the Fourth Division, racking up several clean sheets along the way.

Some of that new-found defensive efficiency was down to Don Howe, who spent several weeks passing on his experience to Fry's boys. You could say they needed it, after losing their first-ever League game 7-4.

"We had three clean sheets in a row at one point," says Barry. "In my 11 years at Barnet I don't think that has ever happened before. Around here, we thought you only got clean sheets from the laundrette."

"I'm a willy-nilly sort of manager," he admits. "I tell my players to go out there and express themselves. I couldn't tell you what my defenders are doing wrong.

"Don Howe was only with us a short time, but my players listened to

BARNET
SHOOT TO KILL

him and they learned from him.

"They were little things he worked on but they made a big difference."

A little club with big ideas, Barnet made the transition from Vauxhall Conference to League football painlessly. They certainly won't alter their free-flowing style whatever the opposition.

The club's success could point the way to the future for sides in the lower divisions struggling on the breadline. The club has only 15 full-time professionals and nine part-timers, allowing Barry to keep the wage bill down.

"Because of their full-time occupations a lot of our lads only come in for training once or twice a week," says Barry.

"Others take off for work the minute we finish training, so really we get away with murder."

Whenever a star name like Gary Bull is sold, Fry taps into the goldmine of non-League football for replacements. It's territory he's well familiar with. He sees no reason for success to change his formula - a formula that normally means goals, goals, goals.

Barry Fry the 'willy-nilly' boss

BARNET'S success story wasn't done by the book, but then with Barry Fry running the show, that was never likely.

"We go out simply with the intention of scoring more than the opposition," says Barry, the man who epitomises Barnet. He hands out the tea after training and often answers the phone at the club's Underhill Stadium. He also manages the team.

His is hardly the traditional approach to management, but it's very straight-forward. "So many go out with the intention of stifling and man-marking the opposition's star players," he says. "We go out simply with the intention of scoring more goals than they do.

"People said my approach is dangerous, but it brings us lots of goals every season and that's what fans pay good money to see. We're not

75 Across – Swedish ace at Highbury

46 Across – Soviet star Kuznetsov

ACROSS

1 He's led two Midlands clubs to League title success (5,6)

7 The reverant home of Gillingham (11)

13 Former Coventry defender now with Grimsby (6,6)

14 England's most capped international footballer (5,7)

17 What a player might suffer after a tackle (4)

18 One of the game's governing bodies...initially (1,1,1,1)

19 European Champions in 1984 (6)

21 One of the greatest Italian players of all time (4)

22 The score before penalties in last year's European Cup Final was Red Star ? Marseille ? (3)

24 Former West Brom player and Newcastle boss (7)

26 Ex-QPR and Newcastle winger now at West Brom (7)

27 He's usually only involved in a game two or three times (7)

31 Former Leeds and Forest defender who followed his dad into management (4)

4 Down – Kamara perhaps

33 McCarthy or Duxbury, perhaps (4)

34 Formed a prolific partnership with Luther Blissett at Watford a few years ago (7)

35 Some referees are prone to do this too much (4)

41 Manchester City speed machine (5)

42 Former Leeds player who should be good for indigestion (6)

43 Some successful players are often described as this (4,6)

45 Former England 'keeper - in short (4)

46 Rangers' Soviet star Kuznetsov (4)

47 Park where the team referred to in 85 Across play (4)

48 How many times Coventry have won the FA Cup (4)

54 Former Chelsea and Dundee United midfielder who sounds very patriotic (3,7)

55 The act of combining two clubs, perhaps (6)

56 Christian name of a famous Watford fan (5)

58 Young Southampton defender (4)

59 Most good goalkeepers are blessed with this (7)

60 Nickname of former Wolves striker and now club big wig (4)

61 A transfer valuation (4)

64 Brothers Tommy and Tony (7)

66 Scoreline by which Liverpool destroyed Crystal Palace in a League game a couple of seasons ago (4,3)

68 The home of Spanish giants Barcelona (3,4)

72 ...ton gate - where you'll find one of the Bristol clubs (3)

74 The Court of Bournemouth on the South Coast (4)

75 Christian name of the Swedish ace at Highbury (6)

76 The game's all square (4)

78 ...ley Park - home of Stockport (4)

82 Liverpool broke the British transfer record to sign him last summer (4,8)

SWORD

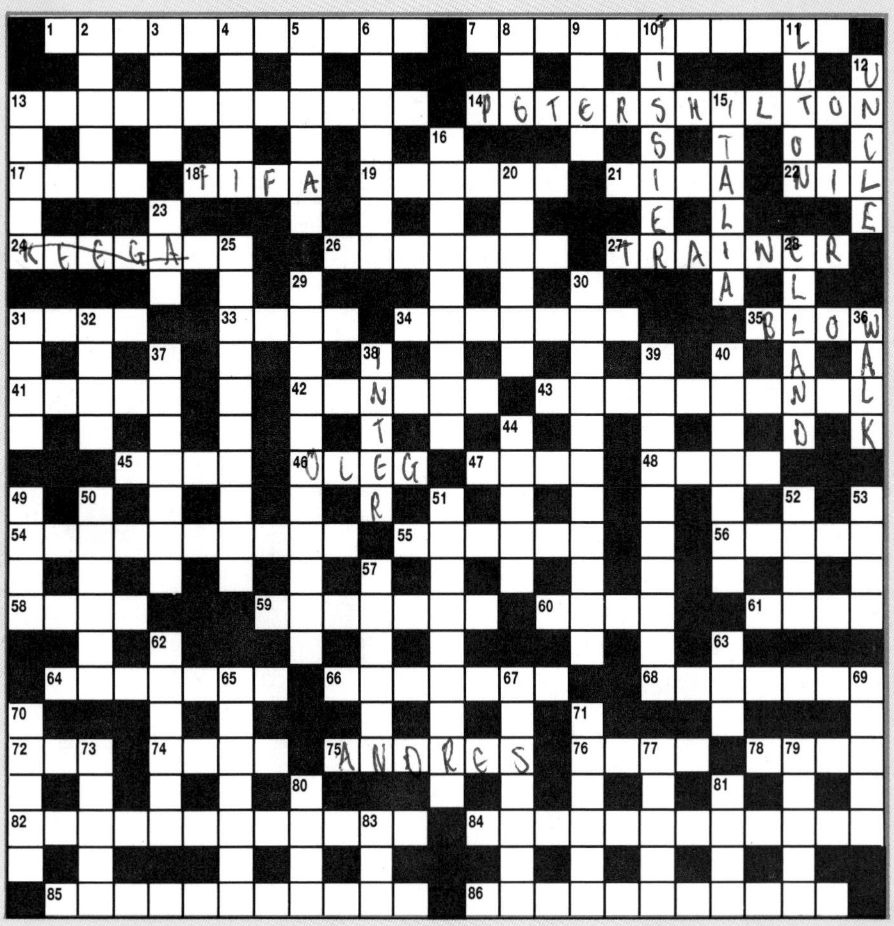

40 Rising star at Charlton who perhaps should be playing baseball (7)
44 Forest, Villa, Spurs and Leeds have been his clubs (5)
49 He's number two to Fergie at Old Trafford (4)
50 Brothers Glyn and Ian (6)
51 Double-winning Arsenal boss (6,3)
52 Word used to describe a club's top player (4)
53 The chirpy cockney in Manchester United's midfield (4)
57 It precedes 'Rovers' but follows 'Bromwich' (6)
62 Nickname of the Bramall Lane club (6)
63 Super, European, World... (3)
65 Bird regularly found at the Goldstone Ground (7)
67 Club which has produced two England managers (7)
69 Where you can read about your favourite team (5)
70 Sweet-sounding company which sponsored Liverpool (5)
71 One of the game's million pound 'keepers (6)
73 He's also known as 'Inchy' (5)
77 Selhurst's bird of prey (5)
79 Dodgy character found at Old Trafford - and it's not Fergie (5)
80 Former Brazilian great who starred in the 1982 World Cup (4)
81 One-time Chelsea hero, now a successful manager (4)
83 Forms the crest of Derby County FC (3)
84 Prolific goalscorer of the Sixties and now a SHOOT favourite (5,7)
85 Nickname of a South Coast club who should be making progress (3,8)
86 A powerful, long-range shot (11)

DOWN

2 King's ..... Tower home of SHOOT (5)
3 Great Dutch side of the 70s (4)
4 Kamara or Kiwomya, perhaps (5)
5 They play at Boundary Park (6)
6 Mansfield defender sounds as though he's up for sale (4,3)
8 Millwall's Scottish midfielder (3)
9 Former Wolves favourite probably played better at night (4)
10 Channel Islander, Le .... (7)
11 There plastic pitch came up in 1991(5)
12 Les Allen, to Clive (5)
13 Football would be hopeless without it (5)
15 Venue for the 1990 World Cup linguistically speaking that is (6)
16 Plymouth powerhouse came from Notts County (4,5)
20 Allan, Ray, Frank...a footballing family(6)
23 Insect you might associate with Brentford (3)
25 Former Liverpool and England hard man (5,5)
28 Road which will lead you to a famous ground in Yorkshire (6)
29 One of the clubs to have benefited from automatic promotion to the Football League (11)
30 Famous Italian coach of the 70s (4,7)
31 He succeeded Terry Butcher as boss at Highfield Road (4)
32 City's Maine man (4)
36 UEFA Cup winner with Ipswich and still going strong (4)
37 Arguably the most skilful player at Ewood Park (7)
38 UEFA Cup winners in 1991 (5)
39 Sunderland's former Celtic defender (5,5)

ANSWERS ON PAGE 125

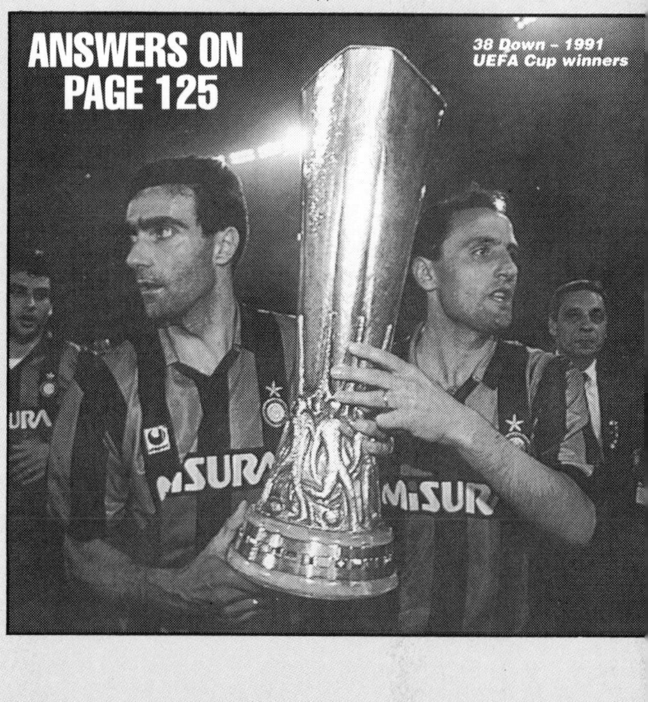

38 Down - 1991 UEFA Cup winners

IN A LEAGUE OF ITS OWN

With the Super League (or Premier League) now a reality, SHOOT takes a walk down memory lane to see how the world's toughest Football League has evolved since William McGregor instigated the idea 104 years ago.

1880's

William McGregor, founder of the League in 1888

'I beg to tender the following suggestion...that ten or twelve of the most prominent clubs in England combine to arrange home and away fixtures each season...'

The words of William McGregor, a proud Aston Villa director, set the wheels in motion for the forming of a Football League. He put pen to paper on March 2, 1888 and sent copies of the letter to Blackburn Rovers, Bolton Wanderers, Preston and West Bromwich.

He received an instant and positive response and on March 23 the five clubs (Aston Villa included) met to consider which other clubs should be invited to join such an alliance.

A second meeting took place on April 17 when it was agreed that 12 clubs should be elected into the Football League. The original five were joined by Accrington, Burnley, Derby County, Everton, Notts County, Stoke and Wolverhampton Wanderers.

Nottingham Forest and Sheffield's The Wednesday, among others, had their claims for membership rejected.

McGregor's foresight was rewarded by his appointment as the first president of the League and on September 8, 1888 the first series of matches between the 12 clubs took place.

All clubs played each other home and away during the inaugural 1888-89 season with two points awarded for a win and one for a draw.

Preston dominated the first competition and took the League title by winning 18 and drawing four of their 22 matches - an unbeaten feat which has never been repeated by a British club in both League AND Cup.

Preston were the first League Champions

The First Day Fixtures			
Sept.8, 1888			
Bolton	3	Derby County	6
Everton	2	Accrington	1
Preston	5	Burnley	2
Stoke City	0	West Brom	2
Wolves	1	Aston Villa	1

How they finished							
(top five)	P	W	D	L	F	A	Pts
Preston	22	18	4	0	74	15	40
A.Villa	22	12	5	5	61	43	29
Wolves	22	12	4	6	50	36	28
B'burn	22	10	6	6	66	45	26
Bolton	22	10	2	10	63	59	22

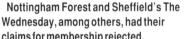

1890's

The First League Champions, Preston, retained the title in 1890 but their supremacy was soon under attack as the competition grew in popularity and expanded.

In 1891 the 12 clubs became 14 and within a further 12 months the League membership had doubled and included a Second Division consisting of 12 clubs.

Automatic promotion and relegation were still years away; instead the bottom clubs in Division One played the top clubs in Division Two (Test Matches) to decide who should play at the highest level the following season.

The system seemed to work until, in 1898, Stoke played Burnley knowing that a draw would ensure both clubs First Division status the next season. Sure enough the result was a goalless draw and, although it smacked heavily of collusion, no charges were brought.

The next season, however, the system of 'Test Matches' was abolished and replaced by automatic promotion and relegation.

The League continued to be dominated by clubs from the North and the Midlands and it wasn't until 1893 that the south was represented in the shape of Royal Arsenal.

But it was Aston Villa, to the delight of League president McGregor, who emerged as the major force and repeated Preston's double-winning achievement in 1897.

Sunderland, admitted to the League in 1890, contested Villa's dominance throughout the decade and over the next seven seasons were beaten just once at home.

Crowds, notably for Cup Finals and crunch League games, had begun to improve during the 1890s with as many as 37,000 filling grounds such as Goodison Park, Everton.

THE CHAMPIONS	
1889-90 Preston	
1890-91 Everton	
1891-92 Sunderland	
1st Division	**2nd Division**
1892-93 Sunderland	Small Heath
1893-94 Aston Villa	Liverpool
1894-95 Sunderland	Bury
1895-96 Aston Villa	Liverpool
1896-97 Aston Villa	Notts Co
1897-98 Sheff.Utd	Burnley
1898-99 Aston Villa	Man.City

Aston Villa emerged as one of the dominant forces of the 1890s

1900's

The 1905 Cup Final between Aston Villa and Newcastle United

In 1904 Royal Arsenal, by then Woolwich Arsenal, became the first London club to play in the First Division.

Still based south of the River Thames (they moved north a few years later) they were promoted from Division Two along with Preston and stayed in the top flight until a disastrous 1912-13 season.

As Liverpool, who won the first of their record 18 titles in 1901, Newcastle, Sunderland and The Wednesday were wrestling for dominance on the pitch, a fight of a different kind was taking place off it.

The Football Players and Trainers Union (formed originally in 1898) had been accepted by the Federation of Trades Unions, but certainly not by the Football League.

In 1909 the conflict between the two parties, and the FA, reached a head with the League suspending the FPTU chairman and secretary. In retaliation, the players called a strike.

Two days before the start of the 1909-10 season, however, the soccer authorities bowed down and the strike was averted.

The Union didn't exert its power too often and the concept of a maximum wage for professional footballers, accepted in 1901, meant that restrictions on players' wages would not be lifted for a further 60 years.

Also in 1909 Nottingham Forest equalled the record for the highest First Division victory - 12-0 against Leicester Fosse. The record, originally set by West Brom, still stands today.

THE CHAMPIONS		
	1st Division	2nd Division
1899-1900	Aston Villa	The Wednesday
1900-01	Liverpool	Grimsby
1901-02	Sunderland	West Brom
1902-03	The Wednesday	Manchester City
1903-04	The Wednesday	Preston
1904-05	Newcastle	Liverpool
1905-06	Liverpool	Bristol City
1906-07	Newcastle	Nott'm F
1907-08	Man.United	Bradford
1908-09	Newcastle	Bolton

1910's

The outbreak of War in 1914 did not help players wages, nor the game itself.

It provided a social climate not at all conducive to watching football and so the League devised a scheme whereby the available money was shared out to help struggling clubs.

The Government allowed the 1914-15 season to be completed amidst subdued atmospheres, typical of which was the 1915 Cup Final between Sheffield United and Chelsea.

There were so many uniformed soldiers in the crowd that the game became known as 'The Khaki Final'.

For the next four years organised football was restricted to regional competitions in and around London, Lancashire and the Midlands - but no money was paid to players and no trophies were won.

Most of the matches played were totally meaningless - apart from one on Christmas Day 1914 when, amidst the conflict and bloodshed, British and German troops staged a 'friendly' football match.

When the League resumed in 1919 both the First and Second Divisions were increased to 22 clubs. There was controversy too.

Just eight games into the 1919-20 season Leeds City were expelled from the League when, under suspicion for making illegal payments, they refused to open their books to the soccer authorities.

Leeds' fixtures were taken over by Port Vale as a turbulent decade reached a close.

THE CHAMPIONS		
	1st Division	2nd Division
1909-10	Aston Villa	Man.City
1910-11	Man.United	West Brom
1911-12	Blackburn	Derby
1912-13	Sunderland	Preston
1913-14	Blackburn	Notts Co
1914-15	Everton	Derby

Sunderland v Aston Villa at Crystal Palace

Sunderland - Cup Finalists in 1912-13

1920's

Herbert Chapman

more responsible than most for changing the face of the game. Enter, the Chapman Era.

Herbert Chapman suffered an undistinguished start to his managerial career when his club, Leeds City, was thrown out of the League for making illegal payments.

Chapman himself was suspended for a while, but returned to the game and became Huddersfield manager in September 1920.

After completing a hat-trick of Championship triumphs Chapman felt he had done all he could for Huddersfield and left to take charge of Arsenal.

His tactics, managerial methods and foresight revolutionised the game, but success didn't come instantly.

THE CHAMPIONS

	1st Division	2nd Division
1919-20	West Brom	Tottenham
1920-21	Burnley	Birmingham
1921-22	Liverpool	Nott'm Forest
1922-23	Liverpool	Notts County
1923-24	Huddersfield	Leeds
1924-25	Huddersfield	Leicester
1925-26	Huddersfield	Sheff.Wed
1926-27	Newcastle	Middlesbrough
1927-28	Everton	Man.City
1928-29	Sheff.Wed	Middlesbrough

With a new decade came a new structure for the Football League which began to undergo drastic change.

Even before the War the success of clubs from the Southern League had led to numerous requests for membership of the Football League. In 1920 it was finally granted.

Inevitably, there were strong protests from the northern clubs who joined the alliance a year later - the Third Division (South) and the Third Division (North) were born.

Some of the junior members struggled, however, to maintain full-time status and disappeared almost as quickly as they arrived on the scene.

A new soccer generation brought with it new characters and one, in particular, was

Huddersfield Town won the League title three times under Herbert Chapman

1930's

The 1930 FA Cup Final saw the beginning of a second period of Chapman domination.

Arsenal's 2-0 Wembley triumph over Huddersfield, Chapman's old club, signalled the start of a glorious era for The Gunners but the end of a glorious decade for the Yorkshiremen.

The following year Arsenal won their first Championship with a record of 66 points that stood until Leeds bettered it by one in 1969.

In the space of five memorable seasons Arsenal won the title four times and finished runners-up to Everton once.

Chapman had built one of the greatest sides of all time, but sadly he didn't live to see them complete a Championship hat-trick in 1935.

He died in January 1934 with Arsenal, typically, top of the First Division. In 1936 the club unveiled the majestic bust of Chapman which still holds pride of place within the marble halls today.

Arsenal won the Championship again in 1938 but much of the magic had died along with Chapman.

One year later, after Everton had secured their second title of the decade, came the outbreak of World War Two. By the time normal, peacetime football returned in 1946 ten members of the great Arsenal side were unavailable. The memories, however, lived on.

THE CHAMPIONS		
	1st Division	**2nd Division**
1929-30	Sheff.Wed	Blackpool
1930-31	Arsenal	Everton
1931-32	Everton	Wolves
1932-33	Arsenal	Stoke
1933-34	Arsenal	Grimsby
1934-35	Arsenal	Brentford
1935-36	Sunderland	Man.United
1936-37	Man.City	Leicester
1937-38	Arsenal	Aston Villa
1938-39	Everton	Blackburn

Arsenal's Hapgood in action against Birmingham at Highbury, 1933

1940's

Any fears that the Second World War would have a detrimental effect on the game of football were soon allayed.

If anything, the interest in the sport was even greater and the late 1940's became boom years for the game with attendances hitting peaks never reached since.

At the height of its popularity in the 1948-49 season football attracted an incredible 41,271,424 fans to League grounds. Attendance figures today are only half that.

The weekly pilgrimage to a Football League ground was part of a Saturday ritual - in any case there wasn't that much else to do. Televisions were only available to about five per cent of the population in the 1940's.

The 1946-47 season went down as the longest in history. Mid-week matches were banned for a time to save fuel and, as a result of severe weather conditions, cancellations meant the season didn't finish until June 14.

In the race for the first Division One Championship since the War, Liverpool, Manchester United and Wolves slugged it out with The Pool eventually winning their first title for over 20 years.

Arsenal, still clinging on to past glories, captured the Championship the following year before Portsmouth picked up the first of two successive titles - the only First Division triumphs in their history.

This was a good time for football, in terms of support at least, but the boom period was shortlived and the 1950's saw the start of a gradual decline in attendances.

THE CHAMPIONS		
	1st Division	2nd Division
1946-47	Liverpool	Man.City
1947-48	Arsenal	Birmingham
1948-49	Portsmouth	Fulham

Portsmouth - League Champions 1948-49

1950's

After Portsmouth's brief flirtation with soccer dominance, Manchester United and Wolves fought it out for the title 'Team of the Decade'.

Wolves it was who led the way into Europe when, having beaten Honved of Budapest in 1954, they were hailed as the 'Champions of the World'.

In answer to that claim came the campaign from France to initiate a Champions' Cup competition. But while it was Wolves who kick-started the first European tournament, it was Manchester United who became our first Football League club to compete.

The previous year the League had banned Chelsea from participating because of fears of fixture congestion.

It was a new and exciting era for the game both at home and abroad, but with it came tragedy in 1958 when United's 'Busby Babes' were victims of the Munich Air Crash.

Eight players were among the dead.

At home, the League was being upgraded once more. In 1958 the Third Divisions North and South were re-arranged into Third and Fourth.

Because of the extra travelling now involved, costs for these lower division clubs were greatly increased.

Also on the financial side, the maximum wage (which stood at only £12 in the 1956-57 season) was on its way out. Its abolition (see next chapter) meant tragedy for the smaller clubs.

Wolves' Johnny Hancocks and Billy Wright with the Championship trophy

Firemen fight the blaze from the tragic Manchester United aeroplane that crashed shortly after take off in Munich

THE CHAMPIONS

	1st Division	2nd Division
1949-50	Portsmouth	Tottenham
1950-51	Tottenham	Preston
1951-52	Man.United	Sheff.Wed
1952-53	Arsenal	Sheff.Utd
1953-54	Wolves	Leicester
1954-55	Chelsea	Birmingham
1955-56	Man.United	Sheff.Wed
1956-57	Man.United	Leicester
1957-58	Wolves	West Ham
1958-59	Wolves	Sheff.Wed

1960's

Johnny Haynes,
Fulham and England

George Best and Denis Law -
Champions with United in 1967

A new decade kicked off in controversial fashion with the abolition of the maximum wage. Within months we had the first £100 per week footballer, Johnny Haynes.

The smaller clubs soon began feeling the pinch. Gateshead were thrown out of the League to make way for Peterborough in 1960 and two years later Accrington Stanley left of their own volition.

Few clubs were helped either by the steady rise in transfer fees. In 1966 Alan Ball became the first player to be transferred between two English clubs (Blackpool and Everton) for £100,000.

But 1966 also saw the biggest single boost the game could receive - England's World Cup triumph on their own soil.

1960 saw the introduction of a new Cup competition, the Football League Cup, to be run along the same lines as the FA Cup but to be competed for by League clubs only.

It was, they said, doomed to failure. But it grew from its sickly childhood into a respected competition with almost the same appeal as the FA Cup.

Many great sides emerged in the 60's, starting with Spurs' double-winning team of 1961 and ending with Don Revie's all-conquering Leeds, Champions in 1969.

In between times Manchester United, having overcome the tragedy in Munich, emulated the achievement of Celtic the year before by lifting the European Cup in 1968.

Their memorable Wembley triumph over Benfica, coming hot on the heels of two Championship triumphs in the space of three years, made them the new giants of English football.

The likes of Law, Best and Charlton were gracing the game as United threatened to dominate for years to come. Bill Shankly and, a few years later, a certain Brian Clough, however, were soon to put a stop to those ideas.

THE CHAMPIONS

	1st Division	2nd Division
1959-60	Burnley	Aston Villa
1960-61	Tottenham	Ipswich
1961-62	Ipswich	Liverpool
1962-63	Everton	Stoke
1963-64	Liverpool	Leeds
1964-65	Man.United	Newcastle
1965-66	Liverpool	Man.City
1966-67	Man.United	Coventry
1967-68	Man.City	Ipswich
1968-69	Leeds	Derby

1970's

Leeds United's Jack Charlton helps goalkeeper David Harvey clear a Stoke attack

Bill Shankly

The 70's began in pretty much the same way as the 60's - with a London club completing the League and FA Cup double.

This time it was Bertie Mee's Arsenal, Charlie George, John Radford, Frank McLintock and all, who matched the achievement of North London rivals Spurs ten years before.

But while Brian Clough and Bill Shankly were busy building Championship-winning sides of their own, the purists were arguing that entertainment was on the wane.

Certainly the goals were not flowing in the way they had during the swinging sixties when, in the 1960-61 season alone, seven clubs managed to score 100 goals in a season.

Incredibly, by 1971, Liverpool were able to finish fifth in the First Division by scoring just 42 goals - an average of only one per League game.

Derby, Champions for the first time in the club's history in 1972, were renowned for their prowess from set-pieces, corners and free-kicks, with Alan Hinton a key figure.

As a result, greater attention was placed on dead ball tactics by other clubs keen to master the art. It worked for Derby again three years later when they triumphed under Dave Mackay.

In 1973-74 the League decided to promote and relegate three clubs instead of two - encouraging, the cynics said, more defensive play.

Towards the end of the 70's, however, 'defensive' was hardly a word you could use for Shankly's Liverpool, Champions three years out of four. Their dominance wouldn't end there.

THE CHAMPIONS		
	1st Division	**2nd Division**
1969-70	Everton	Huddersfield
1970-71	Arsenal	Leicester
1971-72	Derby	Norwich
1972-73	Liverpool	Burnley
1973-74	Leeds	Middlesbrough
1974-75	Derby	Man.United
1975-76	Liverpool	Sunderland
1976-77	Liverpool	Wolves
1977-78	Nott'm Forest	Bolton
1978-79	Liverpool	C.Palace

1980's

Andy Gray scores for Everton against Sunderland in 1985

Liverpool players celebrate after winning the League Championship for a record 13th time in 1982

Changes came thick and fast at the start of the 80's - but they were not all positive.

As the recession took hold, attendances continued to nosedive and clubs up and down the country - including one-time First Division giants Wolves - were feeling the pinch.

Some of them almost went to the wall as the recession, which began in 1979, got progressively worse as the decade went on.

To add to the game's problems, hooliganism was driving fans away from grounds and, in 1985, the Heysel Stadium disaster led to the banning of English clubs from Europe.

The game hit rock bottom, but some steps were being taken to give the game a lift - and the three points for a win system, introduced at the beginning of the 1981-82 season, helped encourage attacking play on the field.

More importantly, in terms of League structure at least, the 1986-87 season witnessed something of a soccer revolution.

For the first time, in order to reduce the size of the First Division to 20 clubs over a two-season period, a system of play-offs was used to determine some of the promotion and relegation issues.

Equally innovative was the decision to promote the Champions of the Vauxhall Conference - non-League's premier division - directly into the Football League.

The first benefactors of this system were Scarborough who replaced Lincoln in 1987.

In the First Division Liverpool continued to dominate, winning the Championship six times during the 80s - completing the double in 1986 - and having their superiority threatened only briefly by Aston Villa, Everton and Arsenal.

THE CHAMPIONS		
	1st Division	**2nd Division**
1979-80	Liverpool	Leicester
1980-81	Aston Villa	West Ham
1981-82	Liverpool	Luton
1982-83	Liverpool	QPR
1983-84	Liverpool	Chelsea
1984-85	Everton	Oxford
1985-86	Liverpool	Norwich
1986-87	Everton	Derby
1987-88	Liverpool	Millwall
1988-89	Arsenal	Chelsea

1990's

Alan Smith in action for Arsenal on their way to becoming Champions in 1990-91

If the 1980's brought with it changes designed to prolong the suspense of promotion and relegation issues, the 1990's saw arguably the most controversial innovation in the game....

ENTER THE SUPER LEAGUE!

Talk of a Super, or Premier League had been prevalent for some years but it was during the 1991-92 season that things reached a head.

The historic announcement earlier this year that the FA Council had approved the break-up of the 104-year-old Football League ended months of negotiations and speculation.

It also gave rise to massive arguments and cries of derision from those sceptical of the motives of its instigators.

The threat of a players' strike threatened to disrupt, not only the 1991-92 season, but the future of the so-called Super League. Indeed the game itself.

Money, needless to say, lay at the root of the dispute. 'The rich clubs will get richer, the poor will get poorer' was the common cry.

Certainly it seemed that way. The Premier League clubs would benefit most from television deals.

Even before the new League came in to being, the game witnessed its first casualty. Aldershot bowed out of the League before the end of the season

Away from the political and financial wrangling, though, the most important issues of the day - **EVENTS ON THE FIELD** - continued to capture everyone's imagination.

Liverpool, so dominant during the 80s, were no longer the number one force in English soccer. Arsenal wrested the Championship from their grasp before Leeds, Sheffield Wednesday and Manchester United staged a rare northern battle.

THE CHAMPIONS		
	1st Division	2nd Division
1989-90	Liverpool	Leeds
1990-91	Arsenal	Oldham
1991-92	Leeds	Ipswich

KING ARTHUR!

Cox will lay the ghost of Cloughie

The ghost of Brian Clough still stalks the corridors inside Derby's 100-year home at the Baseball Ground. But it doesn't scare current leader Arthur Cox.

He knows all about the great days under Cloughie in the early 1970s when the club reached such giddy heights. He also knows how close he came to emulating those achievements of a bygone era.

King Arthur hauled Derby up by their boots and dragged them virtually single-handedly from the depths of the Third Division back into the top flight.

That in itself was an achievement to rank alongside those of Clough, who took Derby to their first ever title in 1972, and his successor Dave Mackay who repeated the trick three years later.

But, just when it seemed he was on course for another title triumph, the backbone of the side which had taken the club to fifth in the First Division in 1989, began to crumble.

The finances provided by Robert Maxwell to breath new life into Derby County had dried up. As everyone knows, money talks. Suddenly it was talking a foreign language which served to drive the likes of Dean Saunders and Mark Wright away from the Baseball Ground.

Had Cox been allowed to build on the success he had achieved and compliment the 'backbone' of Shilton, Saunders and Wright with suitable limbs, Derby could have been up and running again as a title force.

Maxwell, however, put a freeze

Marco Gabbiadini

Paul Kitson

on transfers and, predictably, the rot set in and Derby were relegated back to the Second Division at the end of the 1990-91 season.

But Cox remained undeterred. Lesser managers may have thrown in the towel. He refused to buckle and his persistance, beligerance if you like, was again suitably rewarded.

When the club was put up for sale, local businessman and self-made millionaire Lionel Pickering answered the call and pledged to provide the money to make Derby great again. So far he has been as good as his word.

Last season alone, Cox was allowed to spend more than £5m in his attempt to mould a side capable of laying the ghost of Brian Clough.

He reshaped the defence and filled the hole created by the departure of Mark Wright to Liverpool by signing youngsters Simon Coleman from Middlesbrough and Andy Comyn from Aston Villa.

In midfield, alongside the tireless and tigerish Geraint Williams, he unearthed a potential England star of the future — Paul Williams. But it was up front that Cox made his most telling changes and most dramatic transfer market assaults.

The men he thrust together in a frenzy of outrageous spending, matched only by Blackburn, are the players on whom his hopes are pinned for the future.

Just as Brian Clough had put so much faith in the forward line of Kevin Hector, John O'Hare and Alan Hinton in the 60s and 70s, Cox is now relying on the talents of £4m trio Marco Gabbiadini, Paul Kitson and Tommy Johnson.

Together with Paul Simpson, a comparatively modest signing from Oxford, and the blossoming talent of Paul Williams, they can be the Baseball Ground heroes well into the Nineteen Nineties.

DERBY'S TASTY TRIO

Paul Kitson	from Leicester	£1.3m
Marco Gabbiadini	from C. Palace	£1.1m
Tommy Johnson	from Notts Co.	£1.3m

Tommy Johnson

TOPSY TURVY COUNTY

An at-a-glance guide to how Derby's League fortunes have fluctuated since they first won the League title in 1972:-

Season	Division	Position
1971-72	Div.1	1st
1972-73	Div.1	7th
1973-74	Div.1	3rd
1974-75	Div.1	1st
1975-76	Div.1	4th
1976-77	Div.1	15th
1977-78	Div.1	12th
1978-79	Div.1	19th
1979-80	Div.1	21st
1980-81	Div.2	6th
1981-82	Div.2	16th
1982-83	Div.2	13th
1983-84	Div.2	20th
1984-85	Div.3	7th
1985-86	Div.3	3rd
1986-87	Div.2	1st
1987-88	Div.1	15th
1988-89	Div.1	5th
1989-90	Div.1	16th
1990-91	Div.2	20th

Cox is out to emulate Derby's title triumph in 1975

BYRNE'S FLIGHT

'Budgie' swoops to conquer . . . after getting lost in France

SUNDERLAND goal ace John Byrne went to hell and back before his career was transformed by the Wearsiders' Wembley march.

In fact, less than two years before scoring the goals which turned an FA Cup fantasy into reality, Byrne had thought about quitting the game during a nightmare spell just across the English Channel with Le Havre.

His Irish eyes were definitely not smiling when, having already won a painful battle against a broken leg, he was banished to play with the French club's youth team following a transfer market mix-up.

Before the 1990 World Cup Byrne was convinced he was on his way to Sunderland and told Le Havre he wouldn't be going back to France.

When old Roker boss Denis Smith bought Peter Davenport instead, however, Byrne was forced to return to Le Havre only to find he couldn't get a game because the club had signed two more 'foreigners'.

"It was the lowest point of my career," recalls Byrne who responded by sending faxed SOS messages to every First and Second Division club in England.

His persistence paid off when Brighton brought him home in a £125,000 deal. Financial problems forced The Seagulls to sell their star performer, however, and after a year Byrne finally got his move to Sunderland.

And he hasn't looked back since.

Achievement

He scored in every round of the FA Cup to steer Sunderland to Wembley and, while he insisted "it didn't matter who scored the goals", he had to confess: "Of course I'm proud of that achievement.

"But it was all down to the team and the chances we create. In fact the winner I scored against Norwich in the Semi-Final at Hillsborough was the easiest I'll ever score.

"Easy or not though, it was still the proudest moment of my career."

IT'S A FUNNY OLD NAME

A soccer who's who . . . with a difference

Wimbledon striker Steve Anthrobus

Let us pray

1 Greg Abbott (Bradford)
2 Jason Priestley (Carlisle)
3 Owen Archdeacon (Barnsley)
4 Ian Bishop (West Ham)
5 Phil Chapple (Cambridge)
6 Nicky Cross (Port Vale)
7 Christian Dailley (Dundee United)
8 Brian Deane (Sheff.Utd)
9 Sean Parrish (Shrewsbury)
10 Neil Pope (Peterborough)

Bible banter

1 Graham Abel (Chester)
2 Gareth Abraham (Cardiff)
3 Brett Angell (Southend)
4 Steve Cross (Millwall)
5 Graham Easter (Preston)
6 Joe Jakub (Burnley)
7 Francis Joseph (Fulham)
8 Paul Kane (Oldham)
9 Noel Luke (Peterborough)
10 Damien Matthew (Chelsea)

Have boots, will travel

1 Steve Anthrobus (Wimbledon)
2 Cliff Carr (Stoke)
3 Ray Train (Ex Carlisle/Oxford)
4 Dean Austin (Southend)
5 Chris Morris (Celtic)
6 David Norton (Notts County)
7 Peter VAN de Ven (Aberdeen)
8 Tony Ford (Grimsby)
9 Paul Wheeler (Hereford)
10 Gordon 'Hillman' Hunter (Hibs)

Food for thought

1 Paul Bacon (Charlton)
2 Steve Pears (Middlesbrough)
3 Steve Cherry (Notts County)
4 Jesse Roast (Maidstone)
5 Nigel Pepper (York)
6 Paul Cobb (Leyton Orient)
7 Scott Minto (Charlton)
8 David Currie (Barnsley)
9 Paul Lemon (Chesterfield)
10 Scott Crabbe (Hearts)

Steve Butler (left) and Tony Pounder

Just the job

1 Robert Painter (Chester)
2 Terry Butcher (ex-Coventry boss)
3 Fred Barber (Peterborough)
4 Richard Carpenter (Gillingham)
5 Simon Coleman (Derby)
6 Davie Cooper (Motherwell)
7 Nick Tanner (Liverpool)
8 Calvin Plummer (Chesterfield)
9 Mark Draper (Notts County)
10 Steve Butler (Watford)

Don't bank on it

1 Worrell Sterling (Peterborough)
2 Ian Banks (Barnsley)
3 Brian Borrows (Coventry)
4 Campbell Money (St.Mirren)
5 Stuart Cash (Nottm Forest)
6 Steve Penney (Hearts)
7 Steve Nicol (Liverpool)
8 Tony Pounder (Bristol Rovers)
9 Kevin Bond (Bournemouth)
10 Lee Clark (Newcastle)

Up the garden path

1 Paul Birch (Wolves)
2 Graham Barrow (Chester)
3 Colin Rose (Crewe)
4 Kenny Mower (Walsall)
5 Mark Gardiner (Crewe)
6 Andy Thorn (Crystal Palace)
7 Perry Digweed (Brighton)
8 Paul Mudd (Scarborough)
9 Neil Parsley (Huddersfield)
10 Bob Bolder (Charlton)

City slickers

1 Justin Edinburgh (Spurs)
2 Alan Hull (Leyton Orient)
3 Alan Paris (Notts County)
4 Dwight Yorke (Aston Villa)
5 Dion Dublin (Cambridge)
6 Julian Darby (Bolton)
7 Brian Hamilton (Hibs)
8 Alan Cork (Wimbledon)
9 Jon Sheffield (Norwich)
10 Alan Sunderland (ex-Arsenal)

Darren Peacock

Animal instincts

1 Alan Lamb (Hartlepool)
2 Paul Herring (Rochdale)
3 Steve Bull (Wolves)
4 Peter Swan (Hull)
5 Ruel Fox (Norwich)
6 James Griffin (Motherwell)
7 Peter Haddock (Leeds)
8 Darren Peacock (QPR)
9 Shaun Goater (Rotherham)
10 Warren Hawke (Sunderland)

Legal Eagles

1 Ian Juryeff (Leyton Orient)
2 Brian Honour (Hartlepool)
3 Jimmy Case (Bournemouth)
4 Ian Holloway (QPR)
5 David Crown (Gillingham)
6 Andy Clarke (Wimbledon)
7 John 'Old' Bailey (Bristol City)
8 John Scales (Wimbledon)
9 Brian Laws (Nottm For)
10 Alan Judge (Oxford)

Owen Archdeacon

HAPPY FA

Scot Gemmill celebrates his Wembley triumph

FOREST youngster Scot Gemmill completed a rare family double when he fired the Nottingham club to yet another Wembley triumph last season.

Okay, so the two goals he blasted in a 3-2 win over Southampton did only secure the return to the City Ground of the ZDS Cup.

But to 21-year-old Scot, and Dad Archie in particular, it was a memorable day indeed.

Because 13 years before, the City Ground coach - then an inspirational midfielder himself under Brian Clough - was a member of the Forest team which triumphed over Southampton at Wembley.

Young Gemmill strikes the Forest winner against Southampton in last season's ZDS Final

Scot's dad Archie was part of Forest's League Cup win over Southampton in 1979

Paul Lake - Manchester City

Michael Lake - Sheffield United

MILIES

The competition may have been different - the Football League Cup - but the scoreline was, incredibly, exactly the same..3- 2 to Forest.

Young Scot was quick to point out, however, that the similarities ended there. "Dad didn't score two goals OR get the Man of the Match award," he cheekily pointed out after the Wembley victory in March.

Scot's performance made dad Archie a proud man and justified Brian Clough's decision to stick by the youngster when other managers might have given up on him.

Perhaps Archie's influence was important. More likely was the fact that Cloughie knew all about the problems of having a son on the club books.

Nigel, of course, learned to stand on his own two feet a long time ago. Now Scot is also following successfully in Dad's footsteps.

He's already worn the blue of Scotland for the Under-21s and Dad says: "It's great to see him play for

his country. It was certainly a proud day when he made his debut. I may be a coach at Forest, but I am still a normal dad with normal feelings."

Elsewhere in the game, family ties are strong - although perhaps not as potent as at the City Ground.

The football family Allen is legendary with Clive and now young Bradley following in the stud marks of Dad Les, and cousins Martin and Paul playing their parts too.

But what of the other family affairs.....?

* FERGUSON: Dad Alex and son Darren at Old Trafford;
* REDKNAPP: Bournemouth boss Harry and son Jamie at Liverpool;
* HARFORD: Blackburn number two Ray and his son, Arsenal youngster Paul;
* LAKE: brothers Michael at Sheffield United and Paul at Manchester City;
* McLEAN: managerial brothers Jim at Dundee Utd and Tommy at Motherwell;
* MACARI: Stoke boss Lou and son Michael, a youngster at West Ham;
* McMENEMY: England boss Lawrie and son Chris, the boss of Chesterfield.

And that's just only a few....

GREAT BRITS

John Barnes - selected by all three panellists

TERRY YORATH
(Wales)

What an opportunity. There are so many great players in the British Isles that you'd have to play every week to give everyone a chance. Without knowing who you are playing it is not so easy to decide whether to put the emphasis on all-out attack or go for a more defensive type of team. I'd probably sit on the fence and try to pick a well balanced side capable of piercing the opposition or blotting out any danger. They don't come any better than my first choice goalkeeper and when it comes to scoring goals you can't ignore the claims of Gary Lineker who has a brilliant international record, especially with the right men to feed him.

My British X1 line-up would go like this:

1. **Neville Southall** (Everton)
2. **Gary Stevens** (Rangers)
3. **Stuart Pearce** (Nottm Forest)
4. **Richard Gough** (Rangers)
5. **Mark Wright** (Liverpool)
6. **Gary McAllister** (Leeds)
7. **Gary Speed** (Leeds)
8. **Gordon Strachan** (Leeds)
9. **Gary Lineker** (Grampus)
10. **Paul Gascoigne** (Lazio)
11. **John Barnes** (Liverpool)

HOWARD KENDALL
(Everton)

I'm glad this will probably never really happen to me. When you really think about it, what a fantastic choice of players we have in these islands. There must be about 100 top players who would be worthy of selection. It's not easy to pick a best eleven out of that lot. I would pick a balanced team and just as when I pick my Everton side there is one name who immediately comes to mind. He is an automatic choice. He is, of course, Neville Southall who I believe is the best goalkeeper in Britain. We have some very good 'keepers in our international squads but I believe Nev is in a class of his own.

My starting line-up would be like this:

1. **Neville Southall** (Everton)
2. **Paul Parker** (Man United)
3. **Stuart Pearce** (Nottm Forest)
4. **Trevor Steven** (Marseille)
5. **Mark Wright** (Liverpool)
6. **Paul McGrath** (Aston Villa)
7. **Andy Townsend** (Chelsea)
8. **Paul McStay** (Celtic)
9. **Gary Lineker** (Grampus)
10. **Niall Quinn** (Manchester City)
11. **John Barnes** (Liverpool)

PETER REID
(Manchester City)

I'd go for all-out attack whoever we were playing. So many foreign teams rely heavily on defence - that's not for me. I would prefer to have a reliable defence but be able to bombard the opposition with some heavy artillery. That's why I would have no hesitation in picking our own Niall Quinn. He has matured into a great player. His 6ft 5 ins height makes him a perfect target for crosses but he is also superb on the ground, not only for himself but for feeding others. In case of accident he is also a very good goalkeeper so I would definitely have him in my British X1. Ian Rush would get my vote as his partner.

My eleven would be like this:

1. **Neville Southall** (Everton)
2. **Paul Parker** (Man United)
3. **Stuart Pearce** (Nottm Forest)
4. **Ray Houghton** (Liverpool)
5. **Richard Gough** (Rangers)
6. **Des Walker** (Nottm Forest)
7. **David Platt** (Bari)
8. **Paul Gascoigne** (Lazio)
9. **Niall Quinn** (Manchester City)
10. **Ian Rush** (Liverpool)
11. **John Barnes** (Liverpool)

How did you compare? Does your team match the experts? Why not test your friends?
Putting the SHOOT panel votes into the computer, the team to represent the British Isles would look like this:

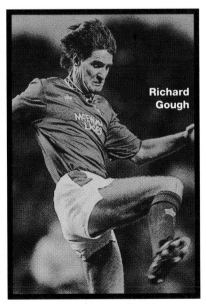

Richard Gough

1. **Neville Southall**
(Everton and Wales)
2. **Paul Parker**
(Manchester United and England)
3. **Stuart Pearce**
(Nottm Forest and England)
4. **Trevor Steven**
(Marseille and England)
5. **Richard Gough**
(Rangers and Scotland)
6. **Mark Wright**
(Liverpool and England)
7. **Gary Speed**
(Leeds and Wales)
8. **Paul Gascoigne**
(Lazio and England)
9. **Niall Quinn**
(Manchester City and Irish Republic)
10. **Gary Lineker**
(Grampus and England)
11. **John Barnes**
(Liverpool and England)

Niall Quinn

Who would be captain? Our panel was split between three names. Stuart Pearce was in the frame and so was Gary Lineker. Finally the choice was Scotland's very own Richard Gough.

Now we're ready to take on the rest of the world!

Ipswich players celebrate their promotion to the Premier League

BUBBLIN

G BLUES

ASK most players about their first senior game, or their debut for their new club or country and they all answer: "I'll never forget it!"

Whatever great moments they enjoy, there is nothing like that first special game. We asked some top stars to tell us about it.

Steve Bruce

The United defender remembers his first game for The Red Devils as being a painful experience but he very nearly didn't make it in to the big time of professional soccer at all.

He'd tried several clubs and just when he was about to give up and become a plumber, he was offered an apprenticeship at Gillingham. His story is now history, but he has a special memory of that first game for United.

"We were playing against Portsmouth and won 2-1. It wasn't a bad game but I felt a bit sore afterwards - I broke my nose. Mind you, I had already broken it five times so I was used to it, but it still gave me a souvenir of the game."

Tony Cottee

The England striker started in even more spectacular fashion.

"My first game was for West Ham against Spurs, we won and I scored. I suppose my debut at Everton was more memorable for me. It was a big step to leave West Ham and go to Goodison. I wanted to do well on my first appearance there. I dreamed of scoring a goal on my debut, but I never expected to get a goal after 34 seconds and then add more to get a hat-trick on my debut for them. I'll never forget that," he says.

Brian Deane

"We were playing against Swansea and I was really wound up for it. I suppose you think it is your only chance. I really gave it everything I had and at the end I nearly collapsed with exhaustion," says the striker on his debut for Doncaster in 1986.

Cyrille Regis

The born-again goalscorer also recalls:

"I made my debut playing for West Brom against Rotherham at The Hawthorns back in 1977. I was very nervous about the game and had just begun to settle when we got a penalty and I was picked to take it. I was frightened to death. Fortunately I scored."

Roy Keane

Brian Clough had a shock in store for the young Irishman.

"I hadn't been at Nottingham Forest very long and I was told that I would travel with the first team to Liverpool for the experience. I was really looking forward to seeing Anfield. I never thought that I would be playing there.

"I was a late choice and although we lost it was fantastic. All the other players were really helpful. My only regret is that I wasn't able to telephone my Dad and get him to come over from Ireland to see the game," says Roy.

Rob Jones

The England full-back had a baptism of fire when he was thrust into Liverpool's first team just 48 hours after joining them from Crewe.

"It was the most frightening day of my life. I was very nervous. I knew it was my big chance to shine in front of the television cameras even though we were playing against Manchester United. I'm grateful to the rest of the lads who helped me get through it," says Rob.

George Hilsdon

Record holder with Chelsea after scoring five times on his debut . He hammered home the goals against Glossop in a 9-2 Second Division match in 1901.

Len Shackelton

Made his debut for Newcastle after being transferred from Bradford Park Avenue and celebrated by scoring six goals on his first outing for the club in a 13-0 win over Newport in 1946.

Fantastic

Alan Shearer

The young England star went into the record books as the youngest player to score a First Division hat-trick and he did it on his full debut!

"It's every Geordie lad's ambition to make the grade as a professional footballer. When I got the chance I wanted it to count. I was nervous but it

Firsts

made me work harder," says Shearer.

"The other Southampton players were really helpful. They knew I was going to be nervous, especially playing against Arsenal. The game seemed to go very quickly and at the end of it I had collected a hat-trick. The lads told me that it was a record. I'll never forget it that day."

Take a look back and discover how well, or badly your team were placed at the end of the 1982-83 season.

FLASHBACK

CHAMPIONS LIVERPOOL BEATEN BY RUNNERS-UP WATFORD!

Saturday May 14th, 1983

FIRST DIVISION

ASTON VILLA (1) 2	**ARSENAL** (0) 1	
Shaw, Gibson	Davis	24,647
COVENTRY (0) 2	**WEST HAM** (1) 4	
Hendrie, Whitton	Goddard, Cottee 2,	
	Swindlehurst	10,919
EVERTON (0) 1	**IPSWICH** (0) 1	
Wark o.g.	Mariner	17,420
MAN.CITY (0) 0	**LUTON** (0) 1	
	Antic	42,834
NORWICH (1) 2	**BRIGHTON** (0) 1	
Channon, Deehan	Smith	20,306
NOTTS CO (1) 3	**MAN.UNITED** (1) 2	
Harkouk 2,	McGrath, Muhren	
McParland		14,414
SOUTHAMPTON (0) 0	**BIRMINGHAM** (0) 1	
	Harford	20,327
SUNDERLAND (0) 1	**WEST BROM** (1) 1	
Chisholm	Thompson	16,376
SWANSEA (0) 0	**NOTTM.FOREST** (2) 3	
	Wallace 2, Anderson	
		9,226
TOTTENHAM (2) 4	**STOKE** (0) 1	
Brazil,	Maguire (pen)	
Archibald 3		33,691
WATFORD (1) 2	**LIVERPOOL** (0) 1	
Patching,	Johnston	
Grobbelaar o.g		27,148

SECOND DIVISION

BLACKBURN (1) 1	**SHREWSBURY** (0) 0	
Garner		3,797
CAMBRIDGE UTD. (0) 1	**OLDHAM** (0) 4	
Sindon (pen)	McDonough 2,Wylde,	
	Henry	3,948
CARLISLE (0) 1	**BARNSLEY** (0) 1	
Robson	Glavin	5,898
CHARLTON (0) 4	**BOLTON** (0) 1	
Hales 2 (1 pen),	Moores	
Gritt, Harris		8,720
CHELSEA (0) 0	**MIDDLESBRO** (0)	
		19,340
DERBY (0) 1	**FULHAM** (0) 0	
Davison		21,124
GRIMSBY (1) 1	**QPR** (0) 1	
Cumming	Stainrod	9,590
LEEDS (0) 2	**ROTHERHAM** (1) 2	
Butterworth,	McBride 2	
Donnelly		14,958
LEICESTER (0) 0	**BURNLEY** (0) 0	
		29,376
SHEFF.WED. (1) 2	**C.PALACE** (0) 1	
Heard, Bannister	Murphy	11,154
WOLVES (2) 2	**NEWCASTLE** (2) 2	
Matthews, Gray	McDonald, Varadi	
		22,446

THIRD DIVISION

BRADFORD C. (2) 3	**HUDDERSFIELD** (0) 1	
McCall, Jackson	Wilson	
Ellis		10,375
BRENTFORD (2) 2	**BOURNEMOUTH** (0) 1	
Joseph, Bowis(pen)	Lee	6,191
BRISTOL R. (0) 1	**CARDIFF** (1) 1	
Platnauer	Gibbins	10,731
CHESTERFIELD (0) 0	**MILLWALL** (0) 1	
	Cusack	4,334
DONCASTER (0) 1	**WALSALL** (0) 3	
Liddell	Roes, Buckley, O'Kelly	
		1,507
LINCOLN (1) 3	**GILLINGHAM** (1) 1	
Shipley, Burke 2	Cascarino	2,241
NEWPORT (1) 1	**EXETER** (0) 1	
Williams	Rogers	3,520
ORIENT (2) 4	**SHEFF.UTD.** (1) 1	
Houchen, Kitchen,	Houston	
Godfrey, Roffey		4,458
PLYMOUTH (0) 0	**PORTSMOUTH** (0) 1	
	Biley	14,173
READING (1) 1	**WREXHAM** (0) 0	
Dixon		5,252
WIGAN (0) 0	**PRESTON** (1)	
	Gowling	7,191

FOURTH DIVISION

BLACKPOOL (1) 1	**HARTLEPOOL** (2) 2	
Serella	Linighan, Dobson	
		2,184
BURY (0) 1	**WIMBLEDON** (2) 3	
Parker	Evans, Downes,	
	Fishenden	6,760
CHESTER (1) 1	**SCUNTHORPE** (1) 2	
Thomas	Graham 2	2,560
DARLINGTON (1) 1	**YORK** (3) 3	
Todd	Byrne, Hood, Walwyn	
		1,668
HEREFORD (0) 0	**PETERBORO** (0) 1	
	Raymont	2,075
MANSFIELD (2) 4	**ALDERSHOT** (1) 1	
Woodhead, Bell	Banton	
Kearney,		
Hutchinson		1,786
PORT VALE (0) 1	**NORTHAMPTON** (2) 2	
Newton (pen)	Coffill, Tucker (pen)	
		6,761
ROCHDALE (1) 1	**HULL CITY** (2) 3	
Martinez	G.Mutrie,Roberts,	
	Marwood	2,659
SWINDON (1) 2	**BRISTOL CITY** (0) 0	
Barnard,		
Pritchard		5,103

GLORY, GLORY DUNDEE UNITED
First title success in their 79 year history

SCOTTISH PREMIER

ABERDEEN (2) 5	**HIBERNIAN** (0) 0	
McNamara o.g.		
McGhee,Cowan,		
Angus,Strachan		24,000
DUNDEE (1) 1	**DUNDEE UNITED** (2) 2	
Ferguson	Milne, Bannon	
		25,000
KILMARNOCK (1) 1	**MOTHERWELL** (1) 1	
Simpson	McClair	1,200
MORTON (0) 0	**ST.MIRREN** (1) 2	
	McDougall 2	2,000
RANGERS (2) 2	**CELTIC** (0) 4	
Cooper,Clark	Aitken, McAdam,	
	Nicholas (2 pens)	
		40,000

FINAL TABLES 1982-83

FIRST DIVISION

	P	W	D	L	F	A	W	D	L	F	A	Pts
			Home					Away				
Liverpool	42	16	4	1	55	16	8	6	7	32	21	**82**
Watford	42	16	2	3	49	20	6	3	12	25	37	**71**
Man. Utd.	42	14	7	0	39	10	5	6	10	17	28	**70**
Tottenham	42	15	4	2	50	15	5	5	11	15	35	**69**
Nottm.Forest	42	12	5	4	34	18	8	4	9	28	32	**69**
Aston Villa	42	17	2	2	47	15	4	3	14	15	35	**68**
Everton	42	13	6	2	43	19	5	4	12	23	29	**64**
West Ham	42	13	3	5	41	23	7	1	13	27	39	**64**
Ipswich Town	42	11	3	7	39	23	4	10	7	25	27	**58**
Arsenal	42	11	6	4	36	19	5	4	12	22	37	**58**
West Brom	42	11	5	5	35	20	4	7	10	16	29	**57**
Southampton	42	11	5	5	36	22	4	7	10	18	36	**57**
Stoke City	42	13	4	4	34	21	3	5	13	19	43	**57**
Norwich City	42	10	6	5	30	18	4	6	11	22	40	**54**
Notts County	42	12	4	5	37	25	3	3	15	18	46	**52**
Sunderland	42	7	10	4	30	22	5	4	12	18	39	**50**
Birm.City	42	9	7	5	29	24	3	7	11	11	31	**50**
Luton Town	42	7	7	7	34	33	5	6	10	31	51	**49**
Coventry City	42	10	5	6	29	17	3	4	14	19	42	**48**
Man. City	42	9	5	7	26	23	4	3	14	21	47	**47**
Swansea City	42	10	4	7	32	29	0	7	14	19	40	**41**
Brighton	42	8	7	6	25	22	1	6	14	13	46	**40**

SECOND DIVISION

	P	W	D	L	F	A	W	D	L	F	A	Pts
			Home					Away				
QPR	42	16	3	2	51	16	10	4	7	26	20	**85**
Wolves	42	14	5	2	42	16	6	10	5	26	28	**75**
Leicester	42	11	4	6	36	15	9	6	6	36	29	**70**
Fulham	42	13	5	3	36	20	7	4	10	28	27	**69**
Newcastle	42	13	6	2	43	21	5	7	9	32	32	**67**
Sheff.Wed.	42	9	8	4	33	23	7	7	7	27	24	**63**
Oldham	42	8	10	3	38	24	6	9	6	26	23	**61**
Leeds	42	7	11	3	28	22	6	10	5	23	24	**60**
Shrewsbury	42	8	9	4	20	15	7	5	9	28	23	**59**
Barnsley	42	9	8	4	37	28	5	7	9	20	27	**57**
Blackburn	42	11	7	3	38	21	4	5	12	20	37	**57**
Cambridge	42	11	7	3	26	17	2	5	14	16	43	**51**
Derby	42	7	10	4	27	24	3	9	9	22	34	**49**
Carlisle	42	10	6	5	44	28	2	6	13	24	42	**48**
C.Palace	42	11	7	3	31	17	1	5	15	12	35	**48**
Middlesbro	42	8	7	6	27	29	3	8	10	19	38	**48**
Charlton	42	11	3	7	40	31	2	6	13	23	55	**48**
Chelsea	42	8	8	5	31	22	3	6	12	20	39	**47**
Grimsby	42	9	7	5	32	26	3	4	14	13	44	**47**
Rotherham	42	6	7	8	22	29	4	8	9	23	39	**45**
Burnley	42	10	4	7	38	24	2	4	15	18	42	**44**
Bolton	42	10	2	9	30	26	1	9	11	12	35	**44**

SCOTTISH PREMIER DIVISION

	P	W	D	L	F	A	W	D	L	F	A	Pts
			Home					Away				
Dundee Utd	36	13	4	1	57	18	11	4	3	33	17	**56**
Celtic	36	12	3	3	44	18	13	2	3	46	18	**55**
Aberdeen	36	14	0	4	46	12	11	5	2	30	12	**55**
Rangers	36	9	6	3	32	16	4	6	8	20	25	**38**
St.Mirren	36	8	5	5	30	18	3	7	8	17	33	**34**
Dundee	36	8	3	7	29	28	1	8	9	13	25	**29**
Hibernian	36	3	11	4	21	17	4	4	10	14	34	**29**
Motherwell	36	9	3	6	28	27	2	2	14	11	46	**27**
Morton	36	4	4	10	14	26	2	4	12	48	30	**20**
Kilmarnock	36	3	7	8	17	31	0	4	14	11	60	**17**

THIRD DIVISION

(How they finished)

Portsmouth
Cardiff
Huddersfield
Newport County
Oxford Utd.
Lincoln
Bristol Rov.
Plymouth
Brentford
Walsall
Sheff.Utd.
Bradford City
Gillingham
Bournemouth
Southend Utd.
Preston
Millwall
Wigan
Exeter
Orient
Reading
Wrexham
Doncaster
Chesterfield

SCOTTISH FIRST DIVISION

St.Johnstone
Hearts
Clydebank
Partick
Airdrie
Alloa
Dumbarton
Falkirk
Raith
Clyde
Hamilton
Ayr
Dunfermline
Queen's Park

FOURTH DIVISION

Wimbledon
Hull City
Port Vale
Scunthorpe
Bury
Colchester
York
Swindon
Peterboro
Mansfield
Halifax
Torquay
Chester
Bristol City
Northampton
Stockport
Darlington
Aldershot
Tranmere
Rochdale
Blackpool
Hartlepool
Crewe
Hereford Utd.

SCOTTISH 2ND DIVISION

Brechin
Meadowbank
Arbroath
Forfar
Stirling Albion
East Fife
Queen of the South
Cowdenbeath
Berwick Rangers
Albion Rovers
Stenhousemuir
Stranraer
East Stirling
Montrose

THE TOP TEN

Weekend May 14th, 1983.

1. **TRUE** - Spandau Ballet
2. **FASCINATION** - Human League
3. **TEMPTATION** - Heaven 17
4. **WORDS** - F.R. David
5. **DANCING TIGHT** - Galaxy featuring Phil Fearson
6. **PALE SHELTER** - Tears For Fears
7. **CANDY GIRL** - New Edition
8. **WE ARE DETECTIVE** - Thompson Twins
9. **OUR LIPS ARE SEALED** - The Fun Boy Three
10. **CAN'T GET USED TO LOSING YOU** - The Beat

OTHER HIGHLIGHTS

* The first wheel clamps (Denver Boots) are introduced in the London Boroughs of Chelsea, Kensington and Westminster.

* London tube driver Christopher Hughes wins the BBC's Mastermind quiz.

* Prime Minister Mrs. Thatcher calls for a General Election on June 9th.

* Boxer Larry Holmes just hangs on to his World Heavyweight WBC title when taken to the full 15 rounds by challenger Tim Witherspoon in Las Vegas.

WHO WON WHAT 1982-83

League Champions - **Liverpool**
Scottish Champions - **Dundee United**
FA Cup winners - **Man United**
FA Cup Finalists - **Brighton**
Scottish Cup winners - **Aberdeen**
Scottish Cup Finalists - **Rangers**
League (Milk) Cup winners - **Liverpool**
League Cup Finalists - **Man United**
Skol Cup winners - **Celtic**
Skol Cup Finalists - **Rangers**

Northern Ireland's

WORLD CUP '94

TARGET

BILLY BINGHAM is hoping to turn back the clock and bring the glory days back to Northern Ireland.

The Irish national boss is hoping that his current crop of players can emulate the achievements of their predecessors in 1982 and 1986 and reach the World Cup finals.

Bingham's boys enjoyed a sensational tournament in Spain in '82 when they shocked the world by reaching the Quarter- Finals.

They followed up that success by again the reaching the final stages four years later in Mexico.

Fortunes

But since then the Irish fortunes have taken a turn for the worst and they have failed to qualify for two European Championships and one World Cup.

But Bingham insists: "I'm not disappointed with the way things have gone - it's just the cycle of events.

"We're a very small nation and I doubt if we have 30 players in the entire Football League, and if we have they're certainly not in the First Division.

"Inevitably there will be vintage years

Kingsley Black

and that was the case in '82 and '86. Since then we've had to completely rebuild."

Since the Mexico World Cup, Bingham has lost players of the quality of Pat Jennings, Martin O'Neill, Sammy McIlroy and, of course, Norman Whiteside.

Only three players remain from that '86 tournament - Mal Donaghy, Alan McDonald and Nigel Worthington - and it takes time to build a new team.

"I've fiddled around with the side and in the last two seasons we've become harder to beat and that's encouraging," says Billy.

"We've got some good young players like Kingsley Black, Gerry Taggart, Michael Hughes and Jim Magilton and I'm optimistic about the future."

Billy's choice of players is restricted because Northern Ireland fall under the UK umbrella which means he is only able to select players born

BILLY

Mal Donaghy – a hero in 1982 and one of the few Irish players from that era still in international action

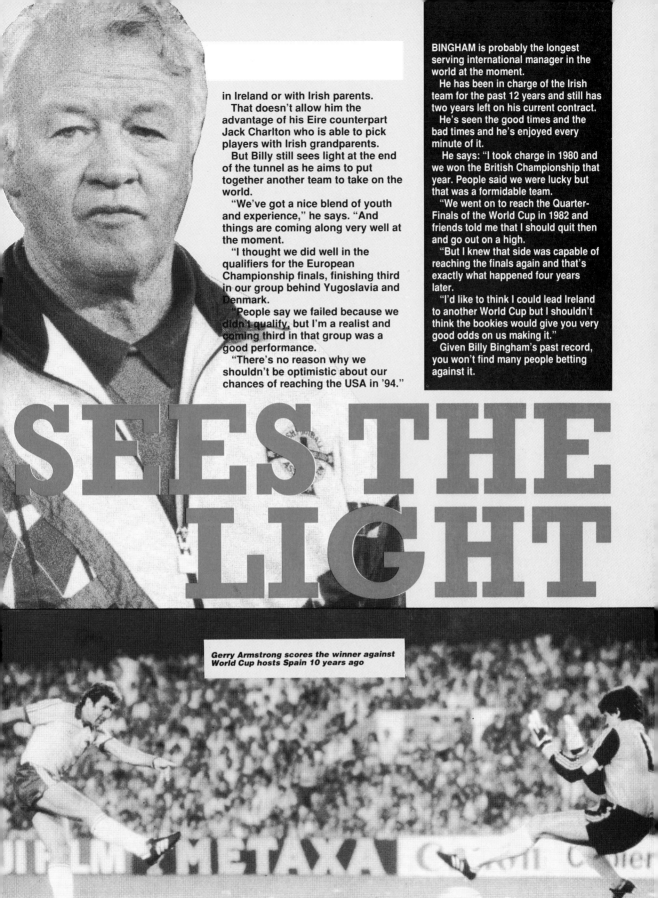

in Ireland or with Irish parents.

That doesn't allow him the advantage of his Eire counterpart Jack Charlton who is able to pick players with Irish grandparents.

But Billy still sees light at the end of the tunnel as he aims to put together another team to take on the world.

"We've got a nice blend of youth and experience," he says. "And things are coming along very well at the moment.

"I thought we did well in the qualifiers for the European Championship finals, finishing third in our group behind Yugoslavia and Denmark.

"People say we failed because we didn't qualify, but I'm a realist and coming third in that group was a good performance.

"There's no reason why we shouldn't be optimistic about our chances of reaching the USA in '94."

BINGHAM is probably the longest serving international manager in the world at the moment.

He has been in charge of the Irish team for the past 12 years and still has two years left on his current contract.

He's seen the good times and the bad times and he's enjoyed every minute of it.

He says: "I took charge in 1980 and we won the British Championship that year. People said we were lucky but that was a formidable team.

"We went on to reach the Quarter-Finals of the World Cup in 1982 and friends told me that I should quit then and go out on a high.

"But I knew that side was capable of reaching the finals again and that's exactly what happened four years later.

"I'd like to think I could lead Ireland to another World Cup but I shouldn't think the bookies would give you very good odds on us making it."

Given Billy Bingham's past record, you won't find many people betting against it.

SEES THE LIGHT

Gerry Armstrong scores the winner against World Cup hosts Spain 10 years ago

PAUL GASCOIGNE has one major ambition in life: "One day I want to play for Newcastle again - with Chris Waddle as manager!"

That's typical of the Geordie spirit, that something special which makes North-East soccer stars always want to "go home".

Wherever he has been, Gazza has never made any secret of the fact that he still likes to spend as much time as possible back home on Tyneside.

His ideal night out is to sink a few Newcastle beers and go for a meal at one of his favourite restaurants in the area. And he's not the only one who kept going back home after he had embarked on a soccer career away from Geordieland.

Chris Waddle had made the move away from Newcastle to Spurs three years before Gazza and warned him at the time: "It'll take time to settle, not because there's anything wrong with being in London or with the Spurs fans, but it is different from Newcastle. I don't think I've ever really adjusted."

He didn't even find it easy to get Newcastle out of his system when he moved to Marseille.

"I still liked to go home whenever there was the chance. My family and friends are mostly still in the North-East. It was even more difficult to

Chris Waddle

Tommy Johnson

settle in France and at first I thought I had made a mistake in leaving Spurs. I was homesick and the language barrier was a problem. I used to worry so much about being unable to communicate with people that I couldn't sleep at nights.

"It was good to be able to go home during the French winter break."

Chris took full advantage of that and used to spend about three weeks on Tyneside, even training with Newcastle.

Tommy Johnson is a Geordie who resisted the chance to star on his home territory.

"I was brought up a Newcastle fan

and used to idolise Kevin Keegan and then Chris Waddle. I wanted to be like them. I think there was some family disappointment when I signed for Notts County, even though the shirt colours were the same. I do not regret that, although I might have done if Newcastle were in a better position.

"Of course, I go back to Newcastle as often as I can and I still miss it but you have to go where your career takes you and perhaps one day mine will take me back to the North-East. I wouldn't hesitate if there was the chance, so long as it was the right move for my career at the time.

There's no place
GEORDIE

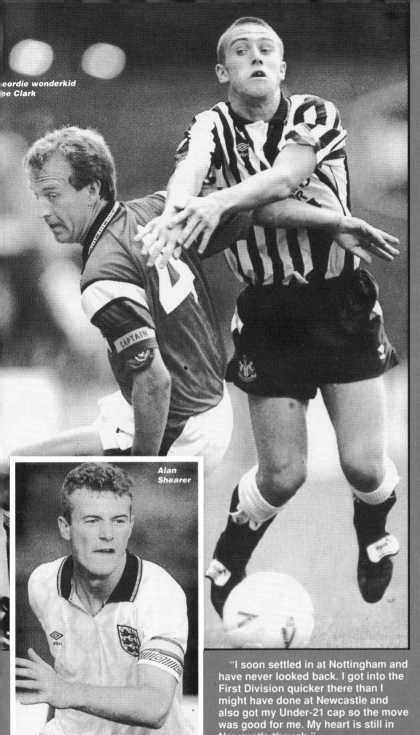

Geordie wonderkid
Lee Clark

Alan Shearer

Bryan Robson, Bobby Robson, Brian Clough, Peter Beardsley, Peter Beagrie, Steve Bruce, Andy Sinton, Barry Venison, Brian Laws, Lawrie McMenemy, Bob Paisley - all big names, all from the North-East.

Lee Clark is one of the young stars who decided to stay with Newcastle, at least while he was making an impression in the game. The Magpies turned down £1.5 million for him while he was still in his teens.

"Obviously I'm ambitious but I want to succeed with Newcastle. I'm happy here and I don't want to leave. It's flattering to know that other clubs are interested in me but I simply don't want to go anywhere else.

"My family live in Newcastle and my friends are here so I'm happy to stay at the club. Anyway, you couldn't find better fans to play for. That's why I signed a contract that would keep me at the club until 1994 and as far as I am concerned I will be happy to sign another one after that."

Try as they might, Newcastle might have been forced to sell their young star by the time this appears in print and if that is the case, Lee will obviously be disappointed but is professional enough to give a new club all he's got.

Exile

But there's another Geordie exile who slipped through the Newcastle net and made his name a few hundred miles away at Southampton. Today he is one of the hottest properties in soccer. He is, of course, Alan Shearer.

"My Dad had me kicking a ball about as soon as I could walk. He was a keen Newcastle fan, as I was, but he did not try to influence me although he would dearly have loved to see me wearing the black and white stripes of Newcastle.

"I had several clubs after me, including Manchester City and West Brom. But I chose Southampton on a hunch. There was no other reason. I did not regret it."

There are countless North-East exiles playing and managing in soccer. They are scattered all over the country and all doing their best for their respective clubs.

One thing they all have in common - they all left their hearts in San Frangeordieland.

"I soon settled in at Nottingham and have never looked back. I got into the First Division quicker there than I might have done at Newcastle and also got my Under-21 cap so the move was good for me. My heart is still in Newcastle though."

The soccer talent that has come from the North-East over the years reads like a who's who of soccer superstars. Bobby and Jack Charlton,

like home for

WEMBLEY

IT IS every player's dream to play at Wembley. Some make it, most don't. Even the great Pele never managed to play on the hallowed turf although he always wanted to. What is it about Wembley that makes it so special?

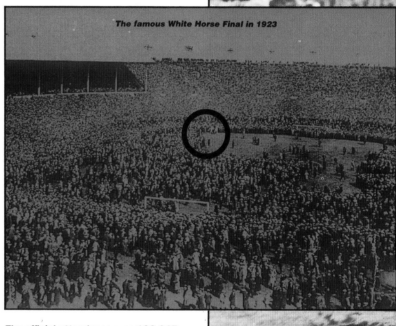

Howard Kendall, now Everton manager, began his visits to Wembley when he was a schoolboy. Little did he know then that it would play such an important part in his life.

"My Dad first took me to Wembley to see the 1958 FA Cup Final between Bolton and Manchester United," he says. "I can remember the excitement of the occasion.

"Wembley had a certain magic and still has. One of the players in the Bolton side that day was Doug Holden. It was amazing that some years later when I played in my first Cup Final we were both in the same Preston side."

On that day - May 2nd, 1964 Howard Kendall became the youngest player ever to take part in a FA Cup Final at Wembley. He was 17 years and 345 days old when he was a surprise choice for the Preston side that lost to West Ham, 3-2.

"You can imagine how I felt. I didn't know that I would be playing until three or four days before the game. The other players were great and helped me to keep calm. It was a fantastic occasion and one I have never forgotten. I have been back to Wembley several times as player and manager and they have all been special memories for me. That's the wonder of Wembley."

Wembley has been soccer's equivalent of the London Palladium since 1923 when on April 28th the mighty stadium opened its doors for the first time with the FA Cup Final between West Ham and Bolton.

The famous White Horse Final in 1923

The official attendance was 126,047 although it was generally agreed that at least another 25,000 'bunked in'.

The effect was incredible as people spilled onto the pitch and the start of the game looked in jeopardy. Then one policeman on a white horse forged his way to the centre of the enormous crowd and began to carve a circle which he gradually widened until the entire pitch was clear and the game could begin.

Within two minutes David Jack scored for Bolton who went on to win 2-0.

There have been some titanic battles at Wembley since then both on the domestic and international soccer scene. Grown men have been seen to cry in their thousands.

Wembley has seen Olympic Games action

WONDERLAND

A young Howard Kendall in Cup Final action in 1964

Leyton Orient even used Wembley as their home ground for two matches during the 1930-31 season when they were Clapton Orient and their new ground was not ready. They played against Brentford and Southend and can truthfully say they have never lost a game at Wembley.

The FA receive about 250,000 written applications for tickets from all over the world before each Cup Final. They have reply letters already prepared in five different languages. Foreign stars get an extra buzz when they hear they are going to play at Wembley. No wonder that England find so many teams rising to the occasion.

There are many plans for new super stadia all over the country but there can never be another Wembley for those who have played there.

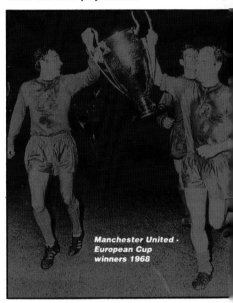

Manchester United - European Cup winners 1968

Who can ever forget the impish jig of Nobby Stiles when England won the World Cup or the tears of joy shed by Bobby Charlton and Matt Busby, air crash survivors who saw their dream come true when Manchester United won the European Cup in 1968?

And Wembley's magic is not just confined to soccer. The most legendary of greyhounds, world champion speedway stars, Rugby League giants, Muhammed Ali, Michael Jackson, military tattoos, the superstars of showjumping, Jehovah's Witnesses, the Olympic Games, the Royal Family - they have all been to Wembley.

Emlyn Hughes has been there for both club and country many times.

"From the minute the whistle blows to finish a Cup Semi-Final and you know you are going to Wembley there is not much else you can think about. You have to keep your concentration on the remaining League fixtures, but Wembley keeps coming into your mind. It dominates your thoughts. It is quite simply *THE* highlight of anyone's career.

"Every minute of the day is special and walking up the tunnel into the stadium with all those people greeting you is an amazing experience. The game always seems to go very quickly and hopefully you find yourself doing a lap of honour if you have just won a Cup or just waving to the fans if it is an international or you have lost.

"Whatever the outcome it is still a fantastic experience. I would rather have gone there every year and lost every time than never have gone there at all," adds Emlyn.

John Harkes (right) was there with Sheffield Wednesday for the 1991 Rumbelows Cup Final against Manchester United. As an American he never expected to be taking part in such an important occasion when he first tried his hand at English soccer. But he knew all about the magic of Wembley.

"Of course, everyone wants to play at Wembley. I never thought I would but when I suddenly realised that I was going to it was quite amazing. I wasn't really nervous until we approached Wembley Way and saw a sea of blue and white. Then it hit me. I was actually going to play at Wembley. Wow!"

Vinny Samways of Spurs had an attack of nerves on his first big day at Wembley.

"I was so nervous walking out onto the Wembley pitch because it was going to be the biggest game of my life. The Cup Final is a one-off and the winners will be the side that performs on the day. Nobody wants to lose at Wembley. Perhaps some people get used to playing there, but not me."

Perhaps one of the coolest guys to play at Wembley is Liverpool's Steve McManaman.

"I played for the England Under-18's against Spain in a warm-up match before a full international against Argentina in 1991. I don't think I was really nervous, but I was fully aware that I was playing at Wembley. Most people only dream about playing there and yet there I was still a teenager and actually playing on that famous pitch. It was a very special occasion and I hope there will be many more like it."

Some people have appeared at Wembley courtesy of the Football League play-offs. Dean Yates played there for Notts County.

Vinny Samways was a Cup winner with Tottenham in 1991

"I had been to Wembley lots of times but playing there was something totally different. I had always been a spectator before and it is nothing like being out there, walking up the tunnel and playing on that pitch where so many famous people have played before you. You don't fully appreciate it at the time but afterwards it really gives you something to think about."

His view of it is not unlike that of Mike Milligan who was there with Oldham in 1990 when his side reached the Final of the then Littlewoods Cup against Nottingham Forest.

WONDERLAND

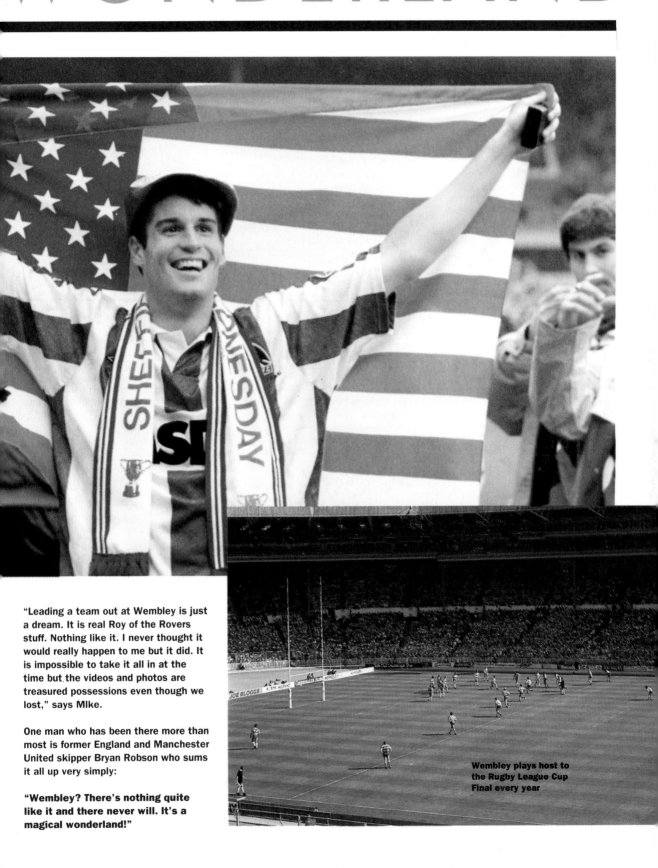

"Leading a team out at Wembley is just a dream. It is real Roy of the Rovers stuff. Nothing like it. I never thought it would really happen to me but it did. It is impossible to take it all in at the time but the videos and photos are treasured possessions even though we lost," says Mlke.

One man who has been there more than most is former England and Manchester United skipper Bryan Robson who sums it all up very simply:

"Wembley? There's nothing quite like it and there never will. It's a magical wonderland!"

Wembley plays host to the Rugby League Cup Final every year

IT'S A GOAL! The scorer jumps for joy - the goalkeeper thumps the ground in despair. A familiar sight and one not enjoyed much by goalkeepers. But they at least have become experts on the deadliest strikers in the country. Here they let you in on the secret of the men they fear...

Peter Shilton rates Paul Mariner as the best

STRIKERS

PETER SHILTON has more experience than any other goalkeeper playing today. He could name an endless list of players who have posed a serious threat to his reputation.

"There have been many over the years and there are as many good strikers today as in the past. People like Lee Chapman, Mark Hughes, Ian Rush all have to be treated with respect. You know they are dangerous. Trevor Francis is still going and he has always been a threat.

"Looking back I think there are few who could beat Kenny Dalglish for ability and I can even recall Jimmy Greaves as being a really top striker.

"If I had to pick one name above all others throughout the years in English football I have to name one who has the edge even over Gary Lineker for me. I'm talking about Paul Mariner. Paul was good in the air, he had pace and the ability to go past defenders to create something out of nothing.

"He had something which every striker needs, the ability to get goals. He was really deadly and would be just as effective in the game today."

BRYAN GUNN of Norwich throws another name into the frame.

"I know there is always plenty to think about when Ian Rush, Mark Hughes and others are bearing down on you. But you would still have to go a long way to find anyone better than Robert Fleck. He is deadly, even in training.

"He's so determined, even in practice matches. He has a terrific shot, a lot of power with his head and is one of those very strong forwards who can take command of the penalty box if you're not careful. That's what he's like in training so I know what other goalkeepers go through against him. He gets my vote."

TONY COTON has faced most of today's top guns while playing for Manchester City. Like most goalkeepers he believes that there are many dangerous players in British football.

"I'd better say first of all that Niall Quinn is pretty dangerous. He puts a few past me in training but I get some consolation from the fact that he also goes in goal when we are training and I

Robert Fleck is Bryan Gunn's top hit-man

Tony Coton Lee Chapman aerial power

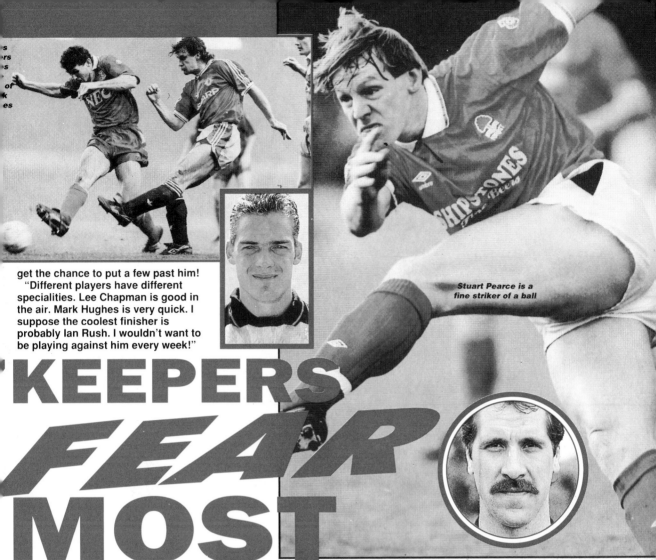

get the chance to put a few past him!

"Different players have different specialities. Lee Chapman is good in the air. Mark Hughes is very quick. I suppose the coolest finisher is probably Ian Rush. I wouldn't want to be playing against him every week!"

Stuart Pearce is a fine striker of a ball

'KEEPERS *FEAR* MOST

Wimbledon's Dutch international goalkeeper HANS SEGERS gives us one of the most independent views of our top strikers.

"Some of the very best goalscorers in Europe are playing in Britain and it is difficult to pick who is the best because on their day they can all turn in great performances.

"For me, the player I least like to face is Mark Hughes. He is one of the very best strikers around and he normally scores past me when we play against Manchester United. I like to see as little of him as possible.

"I can give you a list of players who worry me, but Hughes can score in all different ways from all different angles. He is a goalkeeper's worst nightmare!"

BRUCE GROBBELAAR also knows a good striker when he sees one. He has played behind some of the best. One of his chief threats used to be a team-mate.

"There are two I have always really rated above all others. One is Ian Rush. I'm glad to say that we have only faced each other in training but I have seen how he can destroy the confidence of opposing goalkeepers. I

'Keeper's can't relax with Beardsley around

feel sorry for them sometimes.

"I used to feel the same way about Peter Beardsley but now I feel sorry for myself. Since he went to Everton he has become part of the opposition and playing against us gives him an extra edge. You can't take your eyes off the game for a second when Peter is lined up against you. I'm glad it doesn't happen too often."

DAVID SEAMAN of Arsenal and England is one of the finest 'keepers in the land. He has faced the best today's soccer can offer.

"You have to watch anyone who is in a First Division forward-line and they all have different specialities. Some are threatening in the air while others fire in shots from nowhere and if you are unsighted they can be the most dangerous. Stuart Pearce is not a striker but when you get hold of a shot from him, you know you have something hot to handle.

"I would pick Gary Lineker as being one of the most difficult, but Ian Rush is also one to keep an eye on. For the unexpected you have to watch out for Mark Hughes. When I think about it, there are so many. I think our Ian Wright and Alan Smith take some beating. I'm glad I'm on their side!"

Shoot!

CYRILLE REGIS

CARLTON
PALMER

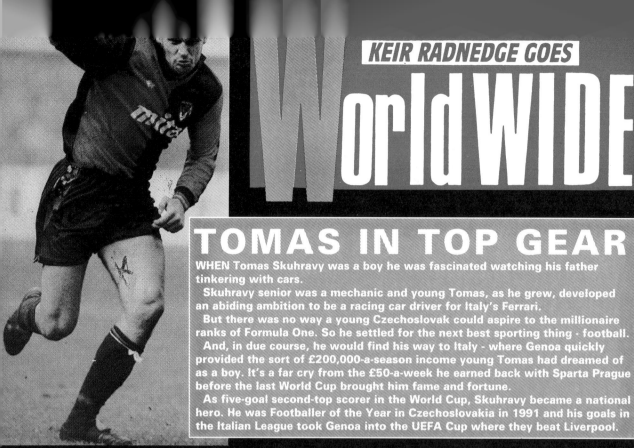

TOMAS IN TOP GEAR

WHEN Tomas Skuhravy was a boy he was fascinated watching his father tinkering with cars.

Skuhravy senior was a mechanic and young Tomas, as he grew, developed an abiding ambition to be a racing car driver for Italy's Ferrari.

But there was no way a young Czechoslovak could aspire to the millionaire ranks of Formula One. So he settled for the next best sporting thing - football.

And, in due course, he would find his way to Italy - where Genoa quickly provided the sort of £200,000-a-season income young Tomas had dreamed of as a boy. It's a far cry from the £50-a-week he earned back with Sparta Prague before the last World Cup brought him fame and fortune.

As five-goal second-top scorer in the World Cup, Skuhravy became a national hero. He was Footballer of the Year in Czechoslovakia in 1991 and his goals in the Italian League took Genoa into the UEFA Cup where they beat Liverpool.

WHEN Paul Gascoigne smashed his knee in the 1991 FA Cup Final, he sent shock waves through not only Tottenham but Italian club Lazio.

Coach Dino Zoff had been relying on Gazza's arrival to spark renewed excitement among the passionate Roman fans.

DOLL FILLS GAZZA GAP

He told his directors: "We cannot wait a year. We must have someone else to fill the gap. Now."

Lazio general manager Carlo Regalia came up with Thomas Doll. Few Italians had heard of him. Now they can't stop talking about him.

In the autumn of 1989 Doll was playing for East German Champions Dynamo Berlin. He played in midfield, in central attack or on the wing. He had played 29 times for the old GDR and expected to be one of their key players in the 1992

European Championship qualifiers.

Then the old Communist regime collapsed, down went the Berlin Wall...and down went the invisible borders which had kept East German footballers from moving West to pick up the lucrative contracts on offer in Western Germany, France, Spain and Italy.

Hamburg, from the West, moved in

quickly. They'd played Dynamo in a friendly and had seen Doll's talent at first hand. A mere £500,000 was enough to seal the deal. And Doll adapted to his new-found football and social freedom so well that quickly he was rated at £2 million. That's what Lazio had to pay for their Gazza-substitute. And they haven't regretted one lira.

SOCCER SHOWMAN

THE OCCASION was a four-team club tournament in Miami two years ago. Atletico Nacional, Colombia's Champions, were beating the United States national team in a friendly.

One man stood out, for both appearance and style: the Nacional goalkeeper, Rene Higuita. With his shoulder-length black, curly hair he looked more like a pirate from the Spanish Main than a footballer.

Up in the stand, watching from his luxury private box, was the stadium's millionaire owner, Joe Robbie. He had built his fortune from picking winners in business. Now he was engaged in picking winners in sport.

Robbie had no doubt.

He said: "I don't know enough about soccer to know how good this boy is from a technical point of view. But he's a showman. If we had a professional league here in the States he would be the first player I'd sign. He'd pack them in."

Robbie's reaction was typical. No-one who has seen Higuita's unique goalkeeping style can remain impassive. He is admired or derided. There is no inbetween.

Indeed, he is not a goalkeeper; rather a goal-sweeper, often roaming far beyond his penalty area to intercept through passes with either foot, chest, or even with a header.

THE BIGGEST...

... ground: **Benfica, capacity 130,000.**

... annual pay cheque: **Robert Prosinecki (Real Madrid), £1.2 million-a-year.**

... transfer fee: **Roberto Baggio, from Fiorentina to Juventus for £8 million.**

... club: **Barcelona - with 105,000 members.**

... caps total: **Peter Shilton (England) 125.**

... international goals total: **Ferenc Puskas (Hungary) 83.**

... career goals total: **Arthur Friedenreich (Brazil) 1,329.**

CRUYFF TAKE OVER

HOLLAND face England in the World Cup qualifiers knowing that, even should they top the group manager Dick Advocaat will be stepping down before the finals.

Even before Advocaat was appointed manager - succeeding Rinus Michels after the European Championships - Johan Cruyff had been named manager if Holland reached the finals.

That may be extraordinary. But it demonstrates Cruyff's charisma - and the power of a personality who has dominated even such a giant club as Barcelona over the past four years.

STEPHEN FROGGATT
(Aston Villa)

Super fit youngster who burst onto the scene in dramatic fashion during the 91/92 season when he got his chance because of injury to wing wizard Tony Daley. Not in the same mould as the 'Daley Express' but Froggatt is no slouch down the left-hand side, and he's capable of scoring spectacular goals - as he proved in last season's FA Cup Fifth Round victory over Swindon.

MARK PEMBRIDGE
(Luton)

A gutsy midfield player with bags of talent - and a nasty streak to match. A product of Luton's youth system, he's been watched by clubs up and down the country for the past year but has handled the publicity well. Managed to shine in a struggling side last season when the highlight for the Merthyr Tydfil youngster was scoring the winner for Wales against the Republic of Ireland in Dublin.

RYAN GIGGS
(Man.United)

Still a kid but has shown maturity beyond his teenage years and, injuries aside, should be a permanent fixture in the United team for much of the decade having signed a long-term contract. Very laid back in his approach, but positive and aggressive on the ball. As in the case of Lee Sharpe, Alex Ferguson has protected him from the media hounds because he knows he possesses the best young talent since Gazza. Current PFA Young Player of the Year.

THE KIDS FOR

CRAIG FLEMING
(Oldham)

A young Scottish full-back who Joe Royle bought from Halifax in 1989. Only 20-years-old, but looks a tremendous prospect and has possibly saved the Oldham boss a fortune after replacing Earl Barrett who moved to Villa for £1.7m in February. He's quick, strong in the tackle and appears to be unaffected by big-match nerves.

Mark Pembridge

A Shoot special on the young stars of '93

CHRIS SUTTON
(Norwich)

His dad Mike played for Norwich and now Chris has completed the family double after an impressive first season in the top flight. Confident, almost arrogant, on the ball, the lanky teenager can play at centre-half or centre-forward. Following the departure of Robert Rosario and the flop of Darren Beckford, Sutton emerged as a useful foil for Robert Fleck last term.

Craig Fleming has been a bargain buy for Oldham

Chris Sutton had plenty to celebrate last term

RICHARD HALL
(Southampton)

Ipswich-born centre-back who joined Southampton from lowly Scunthorpe and made the number five shirt his own with some commanding performances last season. Already being tipped for full international honours, he's powerful in the air and poses a threat to opposing defenders at set pieces. Playing in a team cursed by inconsistency doesn't seem to have rocked his confidence.

FAME

Richard Hall was a Southampton success story last season

ROB JONES
(Liverpool)

Completed one of the most remarkable rises to international status when he made his full England debut against France earlier in the year. Less than six months before he was playing Fourth Division football for Crewe (they also produced David Platt and Geoff Thomas) but shot into England contention when Graeme Souness snapped him up and thrust Jones straight into the Liverpool first team. He looks as though he's been there for years.

RAY PARLOUR
(Arsenal)

George Graham unleashed him onto the First Division scene in dramatic circumstances mid-way through last season when Arsenal visited the scene of their greatest triumph in recent years...Anfield. Unruffled by the occasion - and the TV cameras - Parlour made a promising debut, despite the fact that it was his challenge which gave Liverpool a penalty. Graham has used him sparingly since, but expect him to emerge next season.

Chris Bart-Williams

CHRIS BART-WILLIAMS
(Sheff.Wed)

Surprised everyone, including Wednesday boss Trevor Francis, with the way he adapted to the rigours of First Division football at the tender age of 17. Snapped up from Leyton Orient mid-way through last season, Francis threw him in at the deep end and the gifted midfielder from Sierra Leone wasn't found wanting. Cool and composed on the ball with skill and confidence to spare.

MICHAEL HUGHES
(Man.City)

The Northern Ireland international missed a penalty in only his second appearance for City, but the fact he was prepared to take it says a lot about his character. He has been unaffected by that miss and has gone from strength to strength, making the left-sided midfield role his own. Peter Reid has high hopes for him - and his other City slicker, Michael Sheron.

Part II
Continuing the SHOOT special
on the young stars of '92

THE KIDS FOR

PAUL WILLIAMS
(Derby)

Made great strides last season as he finally justified manager Arthur Cox's faith in him. The Derby boss knew the talent was there, it was just a matter of bringing it to the fore - which Williams (below) did in some style alongside expensive company in the shape of Gabbiadini, Kitson and Johnson.

VINNY ARKINS
(St.Johnstone)

Liam Brady had him lined up to go to Parkhead but the head-strong Irishman, who had already walked out on Dundee United, got fed up waiting for Celtic to find the money and opted for St.Johnstone instead. A prolific scorer in Ireland with Shamrock Rovers his best days as a Premier Division striker are ahead of him.

FITZROY SIMPSON
(Man. City)

Glenn Hoddle rescued him from the soccer scrapheap at Swindon and then provided the platform for him to step up to the top flight with Manchester City. An enthusiastic performer with bags of skill, he's still finding his feet at the highest level but when he does...watch out!

GERRY CREANEY
(Celtic)

With so many strikers on Celtic's books, Creaney (right) kicked off last season well down the pecking order. By the end of it, however, several big names had fallen by the wayside and Creaney was the undisputed number one. A spell of 16 goals in 15 games shot him to the fore as Scotland Under-21s also benefited from his new-found confidence.

SCOTT BOOTH
(Aberdeen)

The youth policy at Pittodrie, so successful under Alex Ferguson and continued by Alex Smith and now Willie Miller, has produced a string of talented youngsters. Under-21 star Booth (below) is one of the picks of the crop which has also yielded international quality in the shape of Eoin Jess and Stephen Wright.

FAME

PAUL KITSON
(Derby)

After hitting the goal trail at Leicester, England Under-21 ace Kitson suddenly found himself being compared with former Filbert Street legend Gary Lineker. So it was perhaps just as well that he escaped the comparisons by moving to Derby for £1.3m earlier this year - money well spent by Arthur Cox.

ANDY AWFORD
(Portsmouth)

Another Pompey player who used the FA Cup stage to project his immense talent - and prove there are few better young defenders in the country...if any. Cool and composed, he was still in his teens during the Cup run but belied his tender years with polished performances throughout, notably against Liverpool in the Semis.

PHIL O'DONNELL
(Motherwell)

The Scotland Under-21 international (below) made such an impact in his first full season that he was labelled the new Bryan Robson and placed in the £1 million class. He turned in some impressive performances for the Under-21s against some of Europe's finest young talent and immediately became a target for PSV of Holland.

SCOTT CRABBE
(Hearts)

A Hearts man through and through, Crabbe was devastated last year when the club threatened to sell him off. The youngster, however, turned down a proposed move to St.Johnstone and vowed to prove the Tynecastle bosses wrong. And he was every bit as good as his word, scoring the goals which took Hearts within an ace of the Scottish Cup and the Premier title.

DARREN ANDERTON
(Tottenham)

Fans at Fratton Park had been singing his praises for some time before 'Shaggy' Anderton (above) arrived on the big screen and made the rest of the country take note. Some breath-taking goals in Pompey's FA Cup run brought him to everyone's attention - not least a host of chequebook waving First Division managers.

ANSWERS

TV Teasers

Chelsea v Everton: 1. Fourth. 2. Allen. 3. Kevin Hitchcock. 4. Tony Cottee - Hitchcock saved it. 5. Graeme Le Saux. Liverpool v Arsenal: 1. Ray Parlour. 2. Jan Molby. 3. Ray Houghton. 4. Michael Thomas. 5. 699th. Man Utd v QPR: 1. Andy Sinton. 2. Three. 3. Peter Schmeichel (Denmark) and Jan Stejskal (Czechoslovakia). 4. McClair. 5. Yes. Sheff Wed v Leeds: 1. Three. 2. Dorigo. 3. Gordon Watson. 4. Substitute. 5. Aston Villa 4-1.

Crossword Answers

Across: 1. Brian Clough. 7. Priestfield. 13. Graham Rodger. 14. Peter Shilton. 17. Ache. 18. ESFA. 19. France. 21. Riva. 22. Nil. 24. Suggett. 26. Fereday. 27. Trainer. 31. Hart. 33. Mick. 34. Jenkins. 35. Blow. 41. White. 42. Rennie. 43. Born winners. 45. Clem. 46. Oleg. 47. Home. 48. Once. 54. Ian Britton. 55. Merger. 56. Elton. 58. Dodd. 59. Agility. 61. Free. 64. English. 66. Nine nil. 68. Nou Camp. 72. Ash. 74. Dean. 75. Anders. 76. Even. 82. Dean Saunders.

Down:
2. Reach. 3. Ajax. 4. Chris. 5. Oldham. 6. Greg Fee. 8. Rae. 9. Eves. 10. Tissier. 11. Luton. 12. Uncle. 13. Goals. 15. Italia. 16. Dave Regis. 20. Clarke. 23. Bee. 25. Tommy Smith. 28. Elland. 29. Scarborough. 30. Enzo Bearzot. 31. Howe. 32. Reid. 36. Wark. 37. Sellars. 38. Inter. 39. Anton Rogan. 40. Pitcher. 44. Hodge. 49. Kidd. 50. Snodin. 51. Bertie Mee. 52. Star. 53. Ince. 57. Albion. 62. Blades. 63. Cup. 65. Seagull. 67. Ipswich. 69. Press. 70. Candy. 71. Seaman. 73. Heath. 77. Eagle. 79. Devil. 80. Eder. 81. Webb. 83. Ram.